WINNING THE BATTLE
AGAINST SIN

HOPE-FILLED LESSONS
FROM THE BIBLE

WINNING THE BATTLE AGAINST SIN

HOPE-FILLED LESSONS FROM THE BIBLE

Fr. Mitch Pacwa, SJ

Published by The Word Among Us Press
7115 Guilford Drive, Suite 100
Frederick, Maryland 21704
www.wau.org

17 16 15 14 13   1 2 3 4 5

ISBN: 978-1-59325-225-0
eISBN: 978-1-59325-450-6

Imprimi potest: Rev. Fr. Timothy P. Kesicki, SJ, Provincial
Chicago-Detroit Province of the Society of Jesus
March 4, 2013

Cover design by John Hamilton Design
Cover art: Lorenzo Ghilberti (1370–1455), "The Temptation of Christ,"
Relief panel from the North Gate, Baptistery, Florence, Italy
Photo credit: Scala/Art Resource, NY

Library of Congress Cataloging-in-Publication Data

Pacwa, Mitch, 1949-
  Winning the battle against sin : hope-filled lessons from the Bible / Fr. Mitch
Pacwa, SJ.
    pages cm
  ISBN 978-1-59325-225-0
  1. Sin—Biblical teaching. 2. Sin—Christianity. I. Title.
  BS680.S57P33 2013
  241'.3—dc23
                        2012047745

To my brother, Jimmy Pacwa, for his fiftieth birthday. From the joy when I heard you were on your way, through the first motorcycle ride I ever gave you, to your present career of customizing motorcycles, I have been delighted to have you as a brother. May God bless you always.

Contents

INTRODUCTION

Sin is a universal phenomenon. We are all born with original sin, and even after we are baptized, we suffer from its effects, finding ourselves attracted to and tempted by actions that are forbidden by God because they harm us and others. For a variety of reasons, however, today these basic truths about sin are not universally recognized. Many have lost their understanding and sense of sin.

One reason is because of the prevalence of moral relativism. If objective truth cannot be known, neither can anyone know what is good or evil, sin or virtue. The best that each person can do is to define his or her own version of good and evil. Of course, this leads to conflicts among individuals and groups who differ about the definition of what is good or evil. Ultimately, a power play will determine the relativists' ideas of moral good and evil: the people with "might" will decide what is "right." In addition, there are also a growing number of people who do not believe in God at all. Without a belief in the existence of God, there cannot be any objective truth about what is sinful and what is not.

Some deny that evil even exists. In a pantheistic worldview, sin and evil cannot exist. The behaviors that other people such as monotheistic Christians and Jews consider sin are then, in fact, not evil at all. They are simply "hard lessons" that people choose to learn, with a result that they will also learn a correspondingly hard lesson when they are reincarnated in another life. Other people are behaviorists who believe that we are determined by our genetics and do not really have the free will to choose either good or evil.

These contemporary ideologies are contrary to most ancient views that sin not only exists but is universal. Ancient people expected both their neighbors and themselves to sin; failures of moral action were assumed to be endemic to every human being. For instance, in ancient Sumer it was taught that "never has a sinless child been born to its mother. . . . A sinless worker has not existed from of old." Akkadian wisdom asserted the same idea: "Who is there who has not sinned against his god? Who that has kept the commandment forever? All humans who exist are sinful."

The Bible also teaches that sin is universal, as seen in the introduction to the flood story: "The LORD saw that the wickedness of man was great in the earth, and that every imagination of the thoughts of his heart was only evil continually" (Genesis 6:5). This verse begins with amazement at the greatness of sin and then moves to the interior quality of this universal evil—"every imagination of the thoughts of his heart was only evil continually." This widespread evil causes God to regret having created human beings.

In the same strain, the Book of Proverbs reflects on the human experience that sin is intrinsic in human life: "Who can say, 'I have made my heart clean; / I am pure from my sin'?" (20:9). This rhetorical question assumes that no one has made his heart clean, nor is anyone pure from sin.

Similarly, in another wisdom book, Qoheleth the Preacher reflects, "Surely there is not a righteous man on earth who does good and never sins. . . . Behold, this alone I found, that God made man upright, but they have sought out many devices" (Ecclesiastes 7:20, 29). Admittedly, Qoheleth is generally cynical about life, but his reflection on the absence of any man who does right and on the mischievous devices of all people has resonated with the experiences of people of faith since he wrote it down early in the second century B.C.

The ancient wisdom, whether among pagans or believers in the one true God of Israel, recognizes that sin is a real experience for everyone, a sad truth from which no individual or society can escape. In this book we will examine the very rich traditions within the Bible to help us define some of the various aspects of sin both in the Old and New Testaments.

The Hope of Our Faith

Why take on such a study? A deeper understanding of this biblical teaching will help us to win the battle against sin that we all face. The truth is that in Christ we have been transformed. Through his passion, death, and resurrection, we have become a new creation. As our faith in this truth grows, we are better able to withstand temptation by standing firm in Christ and the merits of his sacrifice. And if we do fail, we know that through Jesus, we can be forgiven and reconciled. This is the hope of our faith. The aim of this book is to give you a deeper sense of that hope. In studying the biblical passages that follow, you will grow deeper in your faith and also come to a greater realization of the love God has for you and how much he yearns for you to come to him in repentance so that he can grant his forgiveness.

We will begin with the story of the fall of Adam and Eve, not only to see that sin entered the human race at its start, but also to look into aspects of the story of the temptation and fall that pertain to the experience of any and every sinner through the ages. In chapter 2, we will examine why an offense against God is so serious, and in chapter 3, we will seek to understand why we need a divine Savior to reconcile us to God. In chapter 4, we will focus on our responsibility for sin and how our free will gives us a choice for life in Christ or death from sin. Chapter 5 will investigate the Bible's understanding of sin as an experience of slavery and the freedom from sin that we have in Christ. Chapter 6 will discuss the influence of the "flesh" and the ongoing battle between the flesh and the spirit. Chapter 7 will treat the concept of the "world" in the New Testament—the world as the object of God's love and redemption, and the world as an enemy of God and redemption—as well as the influences of Satan. Finally, in chapter 8 we will reflect on God's plan to transform us into the image of his Son.

The last two chapters will give readers the chance to delve into the Gospels and the psalms so that they can meditate on God's love and his invitation to us to come to him to experience his forgiveness and great mercy.

Each chapter begins with a statement of the goal for that chapter as well as a list of the Scripture passages that are treated at length. Each chapter also lists several "takeaway" points to help you understand and grasp the major biblical themes discussed. Finally, each chapter ends with questions for reflection and discussion. These can help you place the themes discussed in the text into the context of your own life situation.

A lengthy discussion of sin goes against the contemporary grain. However, we are often called by God to do what he did, namely, to avoid the wide and easy road so as to take the narrow and hard road that "leads to life" (Matthew 7:13-14). Let us not merely set out on this journey ourselves, but let us invite the world to join us through the narrow gate of life.

THE FIRST SIN

Goal of Chapter 1: *To understand how the first human beings fell from grace and how we fall into the same traps.*

Scripture Highlights: *Genesis 2:25–3:24*

Humans have a desire to understand their origins and roots. Some scientists study the origins of the universe and others study anthropology to understand the origins of the earliest human beings and their cultures. Investigating genealogies on the Internet has even become popular because people want to know more about their family's past. Sometimes it is out of mere curiosity, and other times they want to learn more about inheritances, medical history, or significant patterns in family behavior.

The Bible shows the same interest in origins. The Book of Genesis traces the human family back to the first human beings. Here we are interested in the origin of sin and its effects because these issues continue to plague human existence. The relationship of present-day populations to ancient Semitic genealogies is not so relevant; in fact, most people find those lists to be dry reading at best. However, modern people can look at the stories of sin and find themselves reflected in the various individuals and cultures that still experience the tragedy of human moral failure. A number of approaches can be taken for studying these texts; I would like to propose them as a mirror in which the reader can recognize various components of sinful behavior. This will be quite unlike the magic mirror of the wicked queen in *Sleeping Beauty,* which could compliment the beauty of the visage gazing into it. Like the wicked queen, we may get upset if we recognize that we are not so unlike the sinners recorded in the Bible.

A gaze into this mirror of human frailty may take extra courage in a modern society that prizes self-confidence, positive feedback, and encouraging affirmation. However, St. Ignatius of Loyola, the patron saint of retreat masters, recommends that we make this gaze into the history of human sin in order to discover our own failures and God's mercy as well. In the First Week of his Spiritual Exercises, St. Ignatius summons us to reflect on our own sin by meditating on the biblical stories of sin. However, the goal is not to make us wallow in guilt and remain stuck in it. Rather, we can remember the words of St. Paul: "Where sin increased, grace abounded all the more" (Romans 5:20). St. Ignatius, in fact, instructs us to approach the saving cross of Jesus Christ in full recognition of our sinful state and of the overwhelming grace that Jesus has won for our redemption. The more clearly we come to Christ as sinners, the more powerfully his love and forgiveness enter our being. Therefore, let us not be cowardly in looking at the Bible as a mirror. Let us discover more aspects of our actual image, even with its negative and sinful aspects. Then we can allow God to transform that image into his own image and likeness. That is the purpose of Christ's redemption; let us cooperate with the graces God wants to bestow upon us.

The Story of the Fall

So now let us meditate on the very first sin so that we can see how the first human beings fell from grace and how often we fall into the same traps. Genesis 3:1 describes the serpent with a Hebrew homonym pun from 2:25, the previous verse. While the first couple was naked (*arummim*) and completely innocent of lust, the serpent was the most crafty (*arum*) of all creatures. The words for "naked" and "crafty" come from entirely different Hebrew roots, making the pun itself rather clever.

We begin our reflection on the fall into sin with two points about the serpent. First, note that Genesis 3:1 explicitly states that the Lord God made the serpent; he is not a force equal to God, nor was he made by someone else. Yet the text will show that he is clearly in rebellion against God and will try to spread the rebellion. Second, he is the cleverest of the beasts. This means that we human beings ought never to underestimate how clever the evil one can be in tempting us. Eve proved herself to be naive on this point and fell for his logic; we need to remain alert to his clever ability to convince us to sin.

TAKEAWAY: *Never underestimate how clever the evil one can be in tempting us.*

The temptation is initiated by the serpent. This is necessary since Adam and Eve were still in the state of original innocence and therefore did not have temptation come from within their own mind and will. The same phenomenon appears in the Gospels when Satan tempts Jesus: since Jesus, the new Adam, does not have original sin, he cannot propose a temptation from within his own heart and mind. For those who are without original sin, temptation always comes from outside the person.

The opening sally by the serpent against the woman is to ask her what they both already knew: "Did God say, 'You shall not eat of any tree of the garden'?" (Genesis 3:1). The woman learned her catechism well from Adam; remember that she had not yet been created when the Lord God forbade him to eat of the tree of the knowledge of good and evil (2:15-17). She clearly states, "We may eat of the fruit of the trees of the garden; but God said, 'You shall not eat of the fruit of the tree which is in the midst of the garden, neither shall you touch it, lest you die'" (3:2-3).

Understanding a concept from Israelite anthropology gives us some insight into why the knowledge of good and evil grows on a tree. The ancient Israelites never associated thought with the brain. They considered the brain to be the marrow of the head, related to the senses of seeing, smelling, hearing, and tasting. They believed that they thought with the heart. Acts of the will were connected with the intestines and kidneys; hence, the prophet Jeremiah wrote that the Lord searches the heart and the kidneys (cf. 17:10, usually translated as "mind" and "heart" for modern sensitivities). Given this ancient understanding of the structure of personality, it made sense to describe the knowledge of good and evil as an edible fruit.

The Serpent's Response

The first response of the serpent is typical of many temptations: "You will not die" (Genesis 3:4). The first attack on her solid knowledge of the simple catechism is to deny the punishment. Most people know that bad consequences—otherwise known as punishments—follow upon sin. A key moment in every temptation is to deny these negative consequences. "You won't get caught." "Nothing bad will happen." "Your parents won't really do anything to you." "The police have bigger concerns than your peccadilloes to worry about, so they won't arrest you."

TAKEAWAY: *In the moment of temptation, we often deny the negative consequences of our sin.*

The second tactic taken by the serpent is to attack God's real motive in forbidding the first couple to eat the fruit of the knowledge of good and evil: "For God knows that when you eat of it your eyes will be opened, and you will be like God, knowing good and evil" (Genesis 3:5). The serpent asserts that God has selfish motives—God does not want human beings to know as much as he does. In fact, the knowledge is so powerful that it has the power to transform mere human beings into gods.

This is an appeal to that specific human ability to understand and reason. People want to know about the world and everything in it. The mind craves to pursue the limits of knowledge and push them back. Therefore, the serpent uses this strength of the human mind to disobey a direct commandment not to know good and evil. In fact, he emphasizes this strength by proposing that the knowledge of good and evil can turn humans into gods. This aspect of the temptation pushes the woman beyond disobedience into hubris, the vanity by which humans reach beyond that which is metaphysically possible for them. The temptation contains within it the doom of its own promise: disobedience of God will so distance the sinners that they will not even be able to properly communicate with him, much less become what he is.

Knowledge attained through disobedience will undo the proper relationship with God. The woman does not even consider this consequence; she only hears a promise of fantastic possibilities.

The temptation now moves from the serpent to the woman. She notes two physical attractions to the fruit of the tree of the knowledge of good and evil. First, it looks good to eat. God never said that the fruit would taste bitter; he had simply ordered the man not to eat it. Now the woman finds the possibility of good taste very appealing. Second, it appears to be a "delight to the eyes" (Genesis 3:6). These physical attractions are common to most sins; the wrongful nature of an action does not remove the pleasant qualities it contains by its own nature. Pinocchio found Pleasure Island to be a lot of fun, at least until he turned into a complete ass.

TAKEAWAY: *Sin can be attractive in appearance even though it's wrong.*

A third attraction of the fruit for the woman was its desirability to make one wise. Just as the taste and beauty remained with the forbidden fruit, so also did the actual knowledge of good and evil. However, God had not wanted humans to become so cognizant of evil; he wanted them to know only good. The knowledge of evil was real knowledge, but God forbade it. So often, people are still tempted to know about many sinful realities by trying them out. Looking at pornography, listening to gossip, and other sins can all be proposed as actions that one ought to try "just to see if it is bad for me." The thinking might be: "Just because Sacred Scripture and the Church say the deed is bad does not mean it is bad for me."

Up until this point, no sin has occurred; temptation has intrigued the woman, and that is all. The sin begins the minute she picks the fruit and eats it. The act of disobedience is accomplished, and she has fallen from grace.

The Results of the First Sin

There are several results of the woman's sin. First, she gives the fruit to her husband who is with her (Genesis 3:6). She draws the man into the same act of disobedience, making sin a social reality. An important point that is often overlooked is that the man is with her at this point. One can only conclude that he had been with her throughout the whole process of temptation. He has said nothing to her at all; he has not warned her against disobeying God's command. He has not refuted the arguments of the serpent at any step of the process. His silence must be construed as complicity, which is brought to fruition when he takes the fruit and eats it. The only positive point to be made is that at least they shared!

TAKEAWAY: *Sin is a social reality; our own sin affects others.*

The result of the fall is not the glorious divinity that the serpent promised. Rather, "the eyes of both were opened, and they knew that they were naked; and they sewed fig leaves together and made themselves aprons" (Genesis 3:7). Now they know both good and evil. Prior to the sin, they only knew the good of naked openness without shame or fear of lust. Now they cover themselves with fig leaves, not because they are suddenly cold, but because their nudity is no longer the simple good of total innocence.

The second result of the sin is that the relationship that the man and woman had with God is affected. "And they heard the sound of the LORD God walking in the garden in the cool of the day, and the man and his wife hid themselves from the presence of the LORD God among the trees of the garden" (Genesis 3:8). Note that here, the Lord God takes the initiative to come to the man and woman; they for their part take the initiative to hide from him. Their shame at knowing good and evil causes them to fear God's presence and has not at all made them equal to God.

"But the LORD God called to the man, and said to him, 'Where are you?'" (Genesis 3:9). Venerable Archbishop Fulton Sheen pointed this out as the most significant question of the whole Old Testament. While human philosophy is man's search for God and meaning in life, the Bible tells the story of God's search for man. God searches out individuals before they search for him: Moses at the burning bush; David among the sheep; the prophet Hosea who was wronged by his unfaithful wife; Amos among the herds; the youth Jeremiah; the priest Ezekiel among the exiles in Babylon; the disciples along the Sea of Galilee; and Saul on the road to Damascus.

Now the man must confront the effects of his fall. He says, "I heard the sound of you in the garden, and I was afraid, because I was naked; and I hid myself" (Genesis 3:10). He has to admit that he fears the Lord God because he is naked. Since he now knows the evil of shame, he has to hide himself from God. The sin of disobedience includes a deeper rupture of the easygoing relationship with God than the man and woman had considered during the temptations. In fact, during the temptation, the idea of shame did not cross their minds; they were quite pleased with their resolve to attain knowledge of good and evil. Now the knowledge of evil brings them shame and hiding.

Though no terms of emotion are used in the text, the tone of the Lord God's response is clearly outrage. First comes a rhetorical question: "Who told you that you were naked?" (Genesis 3:11). The expected answer is "nobody." Then a more pointed question is posed: "From the tree which I commanded you lest you eat from it, have you eaten?" (3:11, my translation). Though my literal translation of the Hebrew word order is clumsy in English, it communicates the rhetorical punch of the text and highlights the main point of the sin: God had given a clear commandment against eating the fruit. Obviously, God already knows what has happened, and his question is in fact an accusation that summons the man to take responsibility for his deed.

The next sequence of events is quite common to human beings: push the blame for sin onto someone else. The man answers the Lord God's question first: "The woman whom you gave to be with me, she gave me fruit of the tree, and I ate" (Genesis 3:12). Note the double blame taking place here. First, the woman is mentioned—she gave me the fruit, so it is her fault. Furthermore, you, the Lord God, put the woman here in the garden, so it must be partially God's fault. Very frequently people say, especially after a sin of the flesh like gluttony or lust, that "God made me this way." We sometimes try to implicate God in our own wrongdoing so as to exempt ourselves from full responsibility for our actions, which contradict the commandments he has given us.

TAKEAWAY: *We often try to blame others—including God—for our sin.*

Then the Lord God asks the woman what she has done. Apparently, God accepts Adam's accusation against the woman. She answers, "The serpent beguiled me, and I ate" (Genesis 3:13). It does not matter to her that she had answered the serpent with full knowledge of God's commandment against eating the fruit of the knowledge of good and evil. She focuses on the way the serpent had suggested the possible benefits of breaking God's commandment and uses that as an excuse.

The Punishment—with the Hope of Redemption

After the "blame game" comes the assignment of punishment for the crime. First, the Lord God turns to the serpent, who has no one else to blame. He registers full responsibility to this most clever animal: "Because you have done this, cursed are you among all beasts and among all animals of the field" (Genesis 3:14, my translation). First, there may be a play on words. While "clever among all animals" was *arum* in 3:1, now the serpent is accursed among all animals, *arur*. Also, the Hebrew idiom "cursed among" means "the most cursed," since Hebrew does not have a proper superlative form of adjectives and must use prepositions to communicate the idea of "most." The first experience of the curse will be to crawl on his belly and eat dust his whole life (3:14). This punishment primarily affects him and his descendants.

The second part of the serpent's curse threatens the serpent and his descendants but also offers hope to the humans. First,

God says, "I will put enmity between you and the woman, / and between your seed and her seed; / he shall bruise your head, / and you shall bruise his heel" (Genesis 3:15). This punishment of enmity with the woman fits the crime of deceiving her in the temptation. This enmity will continue through the generations as humans strike the head and serpents strike the heel.

A very odd component of this curse is that the woman is said to have seed. Throughout the Scripture, it is always the male who contributes the seed to the conception of children, with one exception—the conception of Jesus Christ in the womb of the Virgin Mary. Christians have understood this curse of the serpent as a promise of the Redeemer who will be wounded by Satan in the crucifixion but who will destroy the head of Satan by winning a victory over sin. For this reason, Genesis 3:15 is called the "Proto-Evangelium," the first announcement that salvation would come to the fallen human race. The curse of the serpent contains the hope of human redemption.

Next, the Lord God addresses the woman: "I will greatly multiply your pain in childbearing; / in pain you shall bring forth children, / yet your desire shall be for your husband, / and he shall rule over you" (Genesis 3:16). The woman desired the knowledge of good and evil in order to become like a goddess; now she is cursed with pain and, in particular, the pangs of childbirth. The curse contains a conundrum: she will be attracted or impelled toward her husband, who will make her pregnant, which will lead to the pains of childbirth. Just as her desires for the beauty and taste of the fruit helped drive her to disobedience, so will her desire for her husband lead her now to birth pangs. Furthermore, she who had been created as bone of bone and flesh of flesh (cf. Genesis 2:23) will now experience the humiliation of having her husband rule over her.

The last punishment is directed to Adam. First, God makes this accusation: "Because you have listened to the voice of your wife, / and have eaten of the tree of which I commanded you, / 'You shall not eat of it'" (Genesis 3:17a). God does not deny the influence that the woman had on the man; however, neither does he allow it to become an excuse to exonerate him. The issue that matters is that God had given a commandment, and the persuasion of anyone else to contravene it will not discharge the guilt.

Then God gives the curse. Unlike the serpent who is personally cursed, here the curse is on the ground instead of on Adam, the perpetrator of the crime. However, this curse in Genesis 3:17b-19 has four ramifications for Adam. First, "In pain you will eat of it all the days of your life" (my translation). The word for "pain" is the same one used for the woman's birth pangs. He will have equivalent suffering. Second, "Thorns and thistles it shall bring forth to you; / and you shall eat the plants of the field." The earth will not provide the bounty of the God-planted garden but will force the man to work hard just to acquire the plants of the field. Third, "In the sweat of your face / you shall eat bread / till you return to the ground, / for out of it you were taken." The hard labor of working the ground for food to live on will be a lifelong task, lasting until death. And fourth, "You are dust, / and to dust you shall return." Just as the man was created by taking him from the ground, so shall he return to the same ground and become dust mixed with the rest of the dust.

An epilogue of events follows the cursing. First, the woman is given a name, "Eve," because "she was the mother of all living" (Genesis 3:20). Second, the Lord God shows mercy to the naked and ashamed first pair by making them clothes of animal skins to cover the shame they acquired by knowing good and evil (3:21). Third, the Lord God drives Adam and Eve out of the garden to till the soil. Interestingly, the Lord God admits that one of the goals of the serpent's temptation was met: "Behold, the man has become like one of us, knowing good and evil" (3:22a). This is seen not as a positive accomplishment but as a problem. Therefore, the Lord God wants to prevent the man from eating of another tree, the tree of life, by putting him out of the garden, "lest he put forth his hand and take also of the tree of life, and eat, and live forever" (3:22b).

Eating from the tree of life will be a possibility in the future, but for now, it is not. In the Book of Revelation, the Spirit says to the churches, "To him who conquers I will grant to eat of the tree of life, which is in the paradise of God" (2:7). Revelation also says, "On either side of the river [was] the tree of life with its twelve kinds of fruit, yielding its fruit each month; and the leaves of the tree were for the healing of the nations" (22:2). The tree of life would be the cross of Jesus Christ, the new tree of life and immortality. The cross would redeem human beings and expiate their sin. However, immediately after the fall, while the man and woman were still in the state of sin, they had to be excluded from the tree of life. Therefore, the Lord God put the cherubim and a flaming sword to prevent sinners from eating the tree of life (Genesis 3:24).

TAKEAWAY: *There is hope of redemption after the fall. God never gives up on us.*

Reflection on the first sin, the sin of Adam and Eve, shows us that sin, indeed, is "a big deal." And as we look at their sin in a mirror, we recognize how often we act in the same way toward temptation and sin. In the next chapter, we'll reflect on why any sin against God is serious.

–Questions for Reflection and Discussion–

1. Are you alert to the ways in which Satan might try to convince you to sin? What lies might he use to persuade you to give in to temptation? Has he ever tried to convince you that God didn't have your best interests in mind?

2. Have you ever been tempted to "try out" something sinful, just out of curiosity? What was the result?

3. In what ways can an act of sin by one individual draw others into that sin as well? When have you seen this in society at large? When have you seen it in your own life?

4. Why do we often want to push the blame for our sins on someone or something else? How does that impede us in the long run?

5. How does sin affect our relationship with God? Why does God continue to search for us? How have you seen this in your own life? In the lives of your loved ones?

CHAPTER 2

Why Sin Is a Big Deal

Goal of Chapter 2: *To understand the seriousness of sin. As finite humans, we can never pay back the debt of sin because the offense is against the infinite and eternal God.*

Scripture Highlights: *Matthew 18:23-35; Romans 3:23-26; 5:6-11; 1 Peter 1:17-21; Isaiah 53:5-6, 10, 11*

L ord, how often shall my brother sin against me, and I forgive him? As many as seven times?" (Matthew 18:21). When Peter asked that question of Jesus, perhaps Peter was trying to make himself look good by suggesting an extraordinarily generous number of offers of forgiveness. But Jesus responded to him in a way that took the wind out of this fisherman's sails: "I do not say to you seven times, but seventy times seven" (18:22). "Seven times" became a small fraction of the forgiveness we humans are to offer one another. Christ followed up his answer to Peter with the parable of the unforgiving servant. And while its core message is mutual forgiveness, something we will discuss later in this book, let's first examine another ramification that flows from Jesus' parable. Here is the full text of the parable:

> ²³"Therefore the kingdom of heaven may be compared to a king who wished to settle accounts with his servants. ²⁴When

he began the reckoning, one was brought to him who owed him ten thousand talents; [25]and as he could not pay, his lord ordered him to be sold, with his wife and children and all that he had, and payment to be made. [26]So the servant fell on his knees, imploring him, 'Lord, have patience with me, and I will pay you everything.' [27]And out of pity for him the lord of that servant released him and forgave him the debt. [28]But that same servant, as he went out, came upon one of his fellow servants who owed him a hundred denarii; and seizing him by the throat he said, 'Pay what you owe.' [29]So his fellow servant fell down and besought him, 'Have patience with me, and I will pay you.' [30]He refused and went and put him in prison till he should pay the debt. [31]When his fellow servants saw what had taken place, they were greatly distressed, and they went and reported to their lord all that had taken place. [32]Then his lord summoned him and said to him, 'You wicked servant! I forgave you all that debt because you besought me; [33]and should not you have had mercy on your fellow servant, as I had mercy on you?' [34]And in anger his lord delivered him to the jailers, till he should pay all his debt. [35]So also my heavenly Father will do to every one of you, if you do not forgive your brother from your heart." (Matthew 18:23-35)

The king who settles the accounts begins with a servant who owes a fabulous amount of money—ten thousand talents. A talent was sixty-five to seventy pounds of silver or gold; therefore, he owed at least 650,000 pounds of precious metal, a Fort Knox-type of quantity. If it were gold, and if the amount were calculated at contemporary values, then the servant would owe approximately twenty billion dollars. Though the servant pleads that he will pay it all back, the king knows that the sum is far beyond the ability of a mere servant to earn. In fact, although the king decides to sell him and his family into slavery, even the amount he gets for them all would never come to more than the tiniest fraction of the amount owed. The servant begs his lord for patience and promises to pay him everything. Still knowing that repayment is impossible, the lord has pity on him and forgives him the debt.

An Infinite and Eternal Offense

This part of the passage highlights an important principle for understanding sin: the seriousness of a sin depends on *who is offended* rather than on the offender or the offense. This principle is not thought about very much, but it applies to everyday experiences. I typically use the example of my relationship with my younger brother, Paul. We were three years apart in age but further apart in personality, and we fought a lot as boys. Mom and Dad never cared whose fault it was; we both got in trouble. Not only were they angry that we fought with each other, but they disciplined us for hitting each other because it was the wrong kind of behavior for brothers. However, something I must have learned before I was aware of much is that I could never raise my fist to Mom and Dad. I knew that it was a far worse offense than hitting Paul, even though the action on my part would have been exactly the same. Mom and Dad had a higher status in the family than my brother, so it would have been a much more serious offense.

The same principle applies in civil society. If I were to get into a barroom brawl, I would end up in jail for a night or two, and that would be serious. However, if I attempted to hit the president of the United States, I would end up in federal prison for at least a year. I would not be striking a private citizen in that case, as serious as that might be; I would be striking the president of the United States, a federal crime that is made more serious by the office of the individual I hit.

Not many people today apply this principle to God. Rather, many believe that their sins are so small compared to God's infinity that they do not really matter very much. They tend to think of sinning against God as being similar to stealing a few sheets of paper from the copier, a package of gum from Walmart, or some staples from Office Max. Not only is it not a big deal, but it is part of the corporate budget; the company expects people to steal a little bit. Similarly, God expects people to sin, so many believe it is not a big deal.

However, the parable of the servant indicates that sins against the Lord are in fact big deals—so much so that the mere servant cannot pay back the enormous debt. Similarly, just as an offense against the president of the United States makes the action a federal crime, an offense against the infinite and eternal God becomes an infinite and eternal offense. This means it is impossible for a small, finite human being to pay back the debt of sin, just as it was for the servant. No matter how much effort one makes, no matter how many good deeds one does, these will never make up for sin against God. As in the parable, only two options are possible: punishment for the rest of one's existence (which is hell) or mercy from the Lord.

TAKEAWAY: *The seriousness of sin depends on who is offended rather than on the offense. When God is offended, we can't pay back the debt of sin.*

Forgiveness through the Cross of Christ

This parable does not explain the ramifications of the Lord's mercy, but other parts of the New Testament do. The basic message of the New Testament is that we receive forgiveness of sins and reconciliation from God through the death of Jesus Christ on the cross:

> [23]Since all have sinned and fall short of the glory of God, [24]they are justified by his grace as a gift, through the redemption which is in Christ Jesus, [25]whom God put forward as an expiation by his blood, to be received by faith. This was to show God's righteousness, because in his divine forbearance he had passed over former sins; [26]it was to prove at the present time that he himself is righteous and that he justifies him who has faith in Jesus. (Romans 3:23-26)

This passage begins with an assertion that sin is universal, as we have seen already in chapter 1, but then it moves immediately to the means of salvation. The "redemption which is in Christ Jesus" is the source of God's freely given grace. This redemption is "put forward as an expiation by [Jesus'] blood." This text uses the term "expiation" to show that the shedding of Christ's blood on the cross was sacrificial in nature. Christ's sacrifice shows God's righteousness because by it he "passed over former sins." Yet this phrase raises a question: how is the sacrificial death of Christ a demonstration of God's righteousness? A rich answer to this question is found in a group of passages we will examine below. First, another passage from Romans highlights the fact that God's love is demonstrated in Christ's death for the forgiveness of sins:

> [6]While we were still weak, at the right time Christ died for the ungodly. [7]Why, one will hardly die for a righteous man—though perhaps for a good man one will dare even to die. [8]But God shows his love for us in that while we were yet sinners Christ died for us. [9]Since, therefore, we are now justified by his blood, much more shall we be saved by him from the wrath of God. [10]For if while we were enemies we were reconciled to God by the death of his Son, much more, now that we are reconciled, shall we be saved by his life. [11]Not only so, but we also rejoice in God through our Lord Jesus Christ, through whom we have now received our reconciliation. (Romans 5:6-11)

Romans 5:6 relates directly to the early part of the parable of the unforgiving servant. Just as he was completely unable to repay his enormous debt, so are all people in the same position—we are all weak. Christ died for us in our weakness, and in this way God shows his love for us.

TAKEAWAY: *Because he loves us, Christ died for us in our weakness, while we were still sinners.*

A Reason to Rejoice

This passage gives each Christian a better position than the servant in the parable; he had no previous reason to believe that his lord would be patient or merciful to him. St. Paul tells us that we can have confidence that God loves us even before we approach him for mercy and reconciliation. His love is so great that he offers his own Son as the sacrifice for our sins. As he did in Romans 3:25-26, St. Paul again shows us in Romans 5:9 that the blood of Christ justifies us and saves us from God's wrath. This means that we sinners are "reconciled to God by the death of his Son," and we shall be "saved by his life," which continues in the resurrection (5:10). This passage invites each of us to let ourselves own up more honestly and responsibly for our sins, knowing that reconciliation through Christ's death on the cross is a reason to rejoice. Trying to justify ourselves through denial of our guilt and responsibility for wrongdoing simply imprisons us. Straightforward confession of sin and faith in the power of Christ's death to forgive it is the source of Christian life.

The same message also appears at the beginning of Ephesians: "In him we have redemption through his blood, the forgiveness of our trespasses, according to the riches of his grace which he lavished upon us" (1:7-8). Redemption is again the forgiveness of sins. It is a gift to us through Christ's blood, shed on the cross according to God's lavish grace. As in the preceding passages, humans cannot earn this forgiveness; it is a gift of God's grace.

TAKEAWAY: *Owning up honestly to our sins and taking responsibility for them frees us and saves us.*

St. Peter's first epistle also contains rich teaching on the power of Christ's death to reconcile the world's sinners to God.

[17]And if you invoke as Father him who judges each one impartially according to his deeds, conduct yourselves with fear throughout the time of your exile. [18]You know that you were ransomed from the futile ways inherited from your fathers, not with perishable things such as silver or gold, [19]but with the precious blood of Christ, like that of a lamb without blemish or spot. [20]He was destined before the foundation of the world but was made manifest at the end of the times for your sake. [21]Through him you have confidence in God, who raised him from the dead and gave him glory, so that your faith and hope are in God. (1 Peter 1:17-21)

As in the parable of the servant, St. Peter begins with the premise that God the Father is a judge of each and every person. He will judge impartially, evaluating each person's deeds as he lives in this world. This is itself a call to take this life very seriously. Peter also recognizes the universality of sin, pointing out that people inherit "futile ways" of living from their ancestors. However, the good news is that each person can be saved from these ways. Silver, gold, and other items valuable to society do not save anyone. God has created all the precious metals that exist; how can any human offer him enough to pay for past sins? It is as impossible for us today as it was for the unforgiving servant to pay his enormous debt. However, something more precious than silver or gold has been offered: the blood of Christ. He is as innocent as a lamb, unlike any of us sinners, as prophecies of the suffering Messiah indicate:

⁵But he was wounded for our transgressions,
    he was bruised for our iniquities;
upon him was the chastisement that made us whole,
    and with his stripes we are healed.
⁶All we like sheep have gone astray;
    we have turned every one to his own way;
and the Lord has laid on him
    the iniquity of us all. . . .

¹⁰Yet it was the will of the Lord to bruise him;
    he has put him to grief;
when he makes himself an offering for sin,
    he shall see his offspring . . . ;
¹¹he shall see the fruit of the travail of his soul and be satisfied;
    by his knowledge shall the righteous one, my servant,
make many to be accounted righteous;
    and he shall bear their iniquities. (Isaiah 53:5-6, 10, 11)

Since his suffering and death were part of God's plan for our redemption, we sinners are able to "have confidence in God" because he also raised Christ from the dead and "gave him glory" (1 Peter 1:21). This calls for a response in faith and hope, exactly as St. Paul teaches us.

TAKEAWAY: *We can have confidence in the blood of Christ, the innocent Lamb, to forgive our sins.*

St. Peter later restates the teaching that Christ died for sinners: "For Christ also died for sins once for all, the righteous for the unrighteous, that he might bring us to God, being put to death in the flesh but made alive in the spirit" (1 Peter 3:18). The emphasis here is that Christ's death for sins was effective because he was righteous. This death not only forgives sins but reconciles those who are morally unlike Christ—the unrighteous are brought back to God through this death.

Other passages also continue this teaching about Christ's death, including John's first epistle (1 John 2:1-2; 3:16; 4:10-11). In the vision recounted in the Book of Revelation, John begins to weep because no one has been found worthy to open the scroll he sees. However, he is told to stop weeping because "the Lion of the tribe of Judah, the Root of David, has conquered, so that he can open the scroll and its seven seals" (5:5). Then John sees "a Lamb standing, as though it had been slain" (5:6), who was able to open the scroll. This Lamb is then praised by the dwellers of heaven as being "worthy . . . to take the scroll and to open its seals" precisely because he had been "slain and by your blood you ransomed men for God / from every tribe and tongue and people and nation" (5:9). His death is not only a ransom from sin for anyone in the whole world, but it is powerful enough to bestow upon the redeemed a new identity, namely, becoming "a kingdom and priests to our God, and they shall reign on earth" (5:10).

This repeated profession of faith in the death of Jesus Christ redeeming sinners from God's wrath is also stated in terms of his love for sinners. However, these passages do not quite explain why the death of Jesus Christ is so powerful that it can reconcile any and all sinners in the world. They certainly present Jesus as a righteous man who dies for the unrighteous. Yet exactly why is his death so much more powerful than the deaths of many other good and righteous people throughout history? We will examine that question in the next chapter.

–Questions for Reflection and Discussion–

1. Have you ever thought about the seriousness of sin being dependent on who is offended? How does this concept change the way you view sin against God?

2. Are you ever tempted to believe that your good deeds will make up for your sins, past or present? Why is this concept flawed?

3. Does knowing that you are reconciled to God by the blood of Christ on the cross make you confident that you can go to him with your sins and be forgiven? Why or why not?

4. How often do you struggle with denying your guilt or responsibility for your wrongdoing? How could an experience of God's personal love for you help you to own up to your sins and confess them?

5. Why should we take our life, and our sins, seriously? Why should we have hope in Christ, despite the fact that we are sinners?

CHAPTER 3

Why We Need a Divine Savior

Goal of Chapter 3: *To understand why Christ had to be both human and divine to save us from our sins.*

Scripture Highlights: *Matthew 16:13-21; John 8:24-28; Philippians 2:5-11; Colossians 1:19-23; Hebrews 1:4-14; 2:14; 9:25-26*

In the last chapter, we saw how sin is a great debt against God, one we could not possibly pay back on our own. But God loved us so much, even as sinners, that he sent us his Son to redeem us. Christ could redeem us because of his righteousness. He was the righteous One who died for the unrighteous. But why did we need a savior who was divine? And why is that important for us to understand?

A clue to the New Testament understanding of the power of Christ's death to forgive sins is found in the Gospels. Jesus asks the apostles, "Who do men say that the Son of man is?" (Matthew 16:13). The various answers are all incorrect, so he asks them, "But who do you say that I am?" (16:15). It is not the whole group but Simon Peter who replies, "You are the Christ, the Son of the living God" (16:16). This double answer states both that Jesus is the Christ, which is the Greek word for "Messiah," and that he is also the "Son of the living God." The latter point is especially interesting because Jesus had asked them about the identity of the "Son of man." Peter's answer is an early indication of Jesus' divinity. After some discussion about Peter and his future role in the Church (16:17-20), Jesus introduces a new component to his teaching: "From that time Jesus began to show his disciples that he must go to Jerusalem and suffer many things from the elders and chief priests and scribes, and be killed, and on the third day be raised" (16:21). Jesus links the recognition of his divinity with his coming suffering.

A similar link between Jesus' claim to divinity and his prediction that he will die on the cross is made in the Gospel of John. While Jesus engages people in a dispute during the Jewish feast of Tabernacles, he says to the crowd, "I told you that you would die in your sins, for you will die in your sins unless you believe that I am he" (John 8:24). The Old Testament background of this statement is found in Exodus 3:14-15, when God said to Moses, "I AM WHO I AM. . . . Say this to the people of Israel, 'The LORD . . . has sent me to you.'" While this English translation reads "I am he," the word "he" is not in the Greek, so Jesus is really saying, "I am" (John 8:24); that is, he is applying the divine name to himself. When Jesus says "I am," he is claiming to be the Lord God. After this claim to divinity, Jesus says, "When you have lifted up the Son of man, then you will know that I am he, and that I do nothing on my own authority but speak thus as the Father taught me" (8:28). The point here is that Jesus' claim to divinity comes just before he predicts that he will die on the cross.

This link between Christ's divinity and saving death on the cross occurs elsewhere in the New Testament, such as in this passage from Philippians:

⁵Have this mind among yourselves, which was in Christ Jesus, ⁶who, though he was in the form of God, did not count equality with God a thing to be grasped, ⁷but emptied himself, taking the form of a servant, being born in the likeness of men. ⁸And being found in human form he humbled himself and became obedient unto death, even death on a cross. ⁹Therefore God has highly exalted him and bestowed on him the name which is above every name, ¹⁰that at the name of Jesus every knee should bow, in heaven and on earth and under the earth, ¹¹and every tongue confess that Jesus Christ is Lord, to the glory of God the Father. (Philippians 2:5-11)

St. Paul cites what is considered by many to be an ancient Christian hymn. It is important to note that in Philippians 2:6, Christ was "in the form of God" but did not consider his equality with God something to be held on to. Rather, he "emptied himself" by taking human form and "became obedient unto death, even death on a cross" (2:7, 8). As in the preceding passages, the reference to Christ's divine nature is linked with a mention of his death on the cross. Another passage showing this same pattern is from Colossians:

¹⁹For in him all the fullness of God was pleased to dwell, ²⁰and through him to reconcile to himself all things, whether on earth or in heaven, making peace by the blood of his cross. ²¹And you, who once were estranged and hostile in mind, doing evil deeds, ²²he has now reconciled in his body of flesh by his death, in order to present you holy and

blameless and irreproachable before him, [23]provided that you continue in the faith, stable and steadfast, not shifting from the hope of the gospel which you heard, which has been preached to every creature under heaven, and of which I, Paul, became a minister. (Colossians 1:19-23)

The fullness of divinity dwells in Christ, according to this passage. Then immediately following is the reference to the process of Christ reconciling all things by "making peace by the blood of his cross." In fact, he reconciled the hostile and estranged "in his body of flesh by his death." The requirement placed on the redeemed is that they "continue in the faith," not "shifting from the hope of the gospel."

TAKEAWAY: *Christ's divinity and his saving death on the cross are explicitly recognized and linked.*

The Letter to the Hebrews continues this pattern of linking faith in the divinity of Christ with his saving death when one examines the various parts of the letter. The first chapter of Hebrews makes a strong point of showing the divinity of Christ and his superiority over the angels (1:4-14). The second chapter shifts from the teaching about Christ's divinity in order to present his human nature and emphasizes that in it, he was able to suffer: "Since therefore the children share in flesh and blood, he himself likewise partook of the same nature, that through death he might destroy him who has the power of death, that is, the devil" (2:14).

Having established that Christ has two natures, one divine and the other human, Hebrews makes a long and rich presentation about Jesus being the one true high priest according to the order of Melchizedek (cf. Hebrews 5:10; 6:20). Among the points being made in this argument is that as a priest, Jesus must have something to offer, since the offering of sacrifice is the very essence of priestly ministry. "For every high priest chosen from among men is appointed to act on behalf of men in relation to God, to offer gifts and sacrifices for sins" (Hebrews 5:1). "For every high priest is appointed to offer gifts and sacrifices; hence it is necessary for this priest also to have something to offer" (8:3). What Jesus the high priest offers is himself as a pure, unblemished sacrifice on the cross:

[25]Nor was it to offer himself repeatedly, as the high priest enters the Holy Place yearly with blood not his own; [26]for then he would have had to suffer repeatedly since the foundation of the world. But as it is, he has appeared once for all at the end of the age to put away sin by the sacrifice of himself. (Hebrews 9:25-26)

The Book of Hebrews shows that Christ is truly God (in chapter 1) and that he is truly a human who is able to die (in chapter 2). Hebrews then points out that Christ is the high priest according to the order of Melchizedek, superior in priesthood to the priests from the tribe of Levi, and he is the sacrifice that is offered for sins. In this way, Hebrews also links Christ's divinity with his saving death.

One final link between the divinity of Christ and his death on the cross appears in the passion account from the Gospel of Mark: "And when the centurion, who stood facing him, saw that he thus breathed his last, he said, 'Truly this man was the Son of God!'" (15:39). This proclamation by a Roman officer is all the more remarkable in that throughout the Gospel of Mark, a number of spirits had recognized Jesus as being the Son of God but Jesus had always ordered them to be silent (cf. 1:24-25, 34; 3:11-12; 5:7). Even when he performed miracles, he would order people not to spread the news (cf. 1:42-44). The one time that someone can proclaim that Jesus is the Son of God is at the cross.

Trusting in Christ's Power to Save Us

The New Testament consistently teaches that Christ's death on the cross is the means of salvation. We also saw a pattern that developed from Christ's own teaching, the experience of his death, and the message of St. Paul and Hebrews, namely, that the mention of Christ's divinity is frequently associated with the teaching about his saving death on the cross. So we can conclude that Christ's death brings forgiveness of sins precisely because he is God.

Recall the principle that sin takes its seriousness from the one against whom the sin is committed. Therefore, when we sin against God, the sin takes on an infinite and eternal quality because God is by nature infinite and eternal. This fact creates a dilemma for human sinners: being mere creatures, they are inherently finite and limited. No human being can ever do enough to make up for sins committed against God because the infinite quality of the offense cannot be undone by small, limited people. Adding to the problem is the fact that the Ten Commandments, as well as the rest of Scripture, make it clear that God treats every sin, whether directly against him or against other human beings, as sins against himself. Left to themselves, human beings are in an impossible situation when it comes to reconciliation with God.

The escape from this dilemma is that God the Son chose to become man. Remaining fully infinite God, he also submitted to death on the cross, freely giving himself as a sin offering. Because he is man, he can die; because he is God, his death has infinite value. He is the high priest who, with an infinite will, offers himself as an infinite sacrifice; he is capable of bringing true reconciliation for sins that have infinite value because they offend Almighty God. In this way, the tremendous debt that sinful humans cannot pay but owe to God's justice is paid by God himself.

TAKEAWAY: *Only Jesus Christ, both God and man, could pay the tremendous debt owed to God's justice.*

Because of this truth, every single sinner can have confidence in Jesus Christ that their sins are less powerful than his saving death on the cross. He will eternally exceed the evil deeds people commit. From the very beginning of his ministry, Jesus makes this appeal: "Repent, and believe in the gospel" (Mark 1:15). He continues to ask in every age that we repent of our sins and make an act of faith in his saving death of infinite value in order to receive reconciliation with God and one another.

Repentance means that we accept the fact that our sins are evil and that we choose not to commit them again. The faith for which he asks entails a trust in him to apply the power of his saving death to our sins. Faith includes a confidence that he truly forgives the offenses that we bring to Calvary so that we may have reconciliation with God. We Christians have access to a forgiveness far beyond the remission of the enormous debt of the servant in Jesus' parable of the unforgiving servant (Matthew 18:23-35). Jesus Christ goes far beyond words of remission to an action of self-giving that redefines the meaning of God's love for the human race.

–Questions for Reflection and Discussion–

1. If Jesus asked you, "Who do you say that I am?" how would you respond? Would your response be reflected in the way you live your life?

2. Why is it important that Christ's divine nature and his sacrifice on the cross are linked together in the Scriptures? What would have been the significance of Jesus' sacrifice if he had not been divine?

3. Have you ever confessed a sin but still wondered if God had truly forgiven you? How does the knowledge of Christ's power to forgive all sin—past, present, and future—give you confidence that you really have been forgiven?

4. What does the word "repentance" mean to you? Why is true repentance necessary in the battle against sin?

5. How often do you look at a crucifix and think of God's love for you? How can meditating on the Scriptures in this chapter help you to understand the cross as a powerful sign of God's love?

It's Your Choice: Life or Death

Goal of Chapter 4: *God created us with free will, with the ability to choose good or evil. We can allow God to form and shape us, or we can allow other forces to lead us away from God.*

Scripture Highlights: *Isaiah 29:15-16; Jeremiah 18:1-10; Ezekiel 18:2-4, 19-24; Deuteronomy 30:2-4, 6-20; Hebrews 3:12-14; 10:23-31, 35-39; Matthew 21:28-32*

What does it mean to be human? The story of creation in Genesis gives us a basis for answering that question. First, we see that "God created man in his own image, in the image of God he created him; male and female he created them" (Genesis 1:27). Humans were created to reflect God himself, which we see in specifically human attributes such as the ability to reason and to make decisions through acts of a free will. Because we are created in God's image, we possess an inherent dignity. We are also called to self-giving communion, thereby reflecting the life of the Blessed Trinity of three equal divine Persons in a communion of one Godhead. In addition, we are called to reflect God's image and likeness by living holy and upright lives. "Say to all the congregation of the people of Israel, You shall be holy; for I the LORD your God am holy" (Leviticus

19:2). Jesus makes a similar point in the Sermon on the Mount: "You, therefore, must be perfect, as your heavenly Father is perfect" (Matthew 5:48). By virtue of being made in his image and likeness, God is the moral norm for all people.

Because God has created us with free will, we have the ability to make choices that can either help us reflect God's image more fully or that can lead us away from him. The Bible makes it clear that the choice is up to us. Will we allow God to form us, or will we let other forces shape us—the world, the evil spirit, or our own selfish desires? God is our Creator, and he is the only one who truly knows how to shape human life in his own image and likeness, which is our ultimate purpose. He is truly the potter, and we are the clay.

The Image of the Potter and the Clay

This wonderful image is used several times in the Old Testament. In an oracle from the eighth century B.C., the prophet Isaiah begins with a lament over the people's sinful attitude: "Woe to those who hide deep from the LORD their counsel, / whose deeds are in the dark, / and who say, 'Who sees us? Who knows us?'" (29:15). The people tell themselves that the various sins they commit are a secret and that God does not know what they have done. Using the image of a potter and his clay, Isaiah responds with an accusation: "You turn things upside down! / Shall the potter be regarded as the clay; / that the thing made should say of its maker, / 'He did not make me'; / or the thing formed say of him who formed it, 'He has no understanding'?" (29:16). The people are not in charge of their own fate; in fact, the Lord is fashioning and molding them and has formed them from their beginning. They even assert that the Lord "has no understanding," as if he cannot comprehend what people need to do and be. Their attitude treats the creation of man in God's image and likeness as being of no consequence because God does not really understand what it is like to be human.

Another image of the potter and the clay can be found in the book of the prophet Jeremiah. Between 609 and 604 B.C., Jeremiah was told to go to the potter's house to hear God's word (18:1-2). Jeremiah watched the potter at his wheel (18:3) and noticed that when "the vessel he was making of clay was spoiled in the potter's hand, . . . he reworked it into another vessel, as it seemed good to the potter to do" (18:4). The Lord drew out this lesson:

> 6"O house of Israel, can I not do with you as this potter has done? . . . Behold, like the clay in the potter's hand, so are you in my hand, O house of Israel. 7If at any time I declare concerning a nation or a kingdom, that I will pluck up and break down and destroy it, 8and if that nation, concerning which I have spoken, turns from its evil, I will repent of the evil that I intended to do to it. 9And if at any time I declare concerning a nation or a kingdom that I will build and plant it, 10and if it does evil in my sight, not listening to my voice, then I will repent of the good which I had intended to do to it." (Jeremiah 18:6-10)

Two important aspects of God's relation to human destiny can be seen in this passage. First, the Lord God who fashioned the man from the clay of the ground here describes himself as continuing this activity of shaping people. Just as the potter can reshape a clay vessel into a correct form when it is spoiled, so can the Lord reshape the nation if it becomes ruined through sin and evil. Second, the human clay is not completely passive; people can change from doing evil as much as they can change from doing good. Unlike inanimate clay, they use their free will and make a decision, to which God responds by changing their fate to match their behavior.

In a section of Isaiah (chapters 56–66) that was written sometime after the rebuilding of the Temple in 515 B.C., the prophet writes a passage that belongs in a liturgy of repentance. It starts with an act of faith that the Lord is the only God: "From of old no one has heard / or perceived by the ear, / no eye has seen a God besides you, / who works for those who wait for him" (64:4). The next verses confess the people's sinfulness: "Behold, you were angry, and we sinned; / in our sins we have been a long time, and shall we be saved? / We have all become like one who is unclean, / and all our righteous deeds are like a polluted garment" (64:5b-6a). The confession then returns to an act of faith: "Yet, O LORD, thou art our Father; / we are the clay, and thou art our potter; / we are all the work of thy hand" (64:8). It is rare that God is called "Father" in the Old Testament (Deuteronomy 32:6; Isaiah 63:16), so all the more does it bring out the tender care of God for the people here. In that context of fatherly love, the people confess that they are the clay and he is the potter, an acceptance of what had been told them about God previously.

TAKEAWAY: *God can shape us into his image if we cooperate with him.*

The Role of Individual Responsibility

While early Israelite thought emphasized the role of sin in the community, the importance of the individual's judgment before God eventually became more prominent. The communal sense of responsibility was never lost, but the idea of individual responsibility was emphasized and took hold in New Testament theology as well. Ezekiel 18 addresses the exiles in Babylon, where the prophet also lived, about individual judgment. Through Ezekiel the Lord begins this teaching by challenging the people:

[2]"What do you mean by repeating this proverb concerning the land of Israel, 'The fathers have eaten sour grapes, and the children's teeth are set on edge?' [3]As I live, says the Lord GOD, this proverb shall no more be used by you in Israel. [4]Behold, all souls are mine; the soul of the father as well as the soul of the son is mine: the soul that sins shall die." (Ezekiel 18:2-4)

The Lord explicitly rejects the idea that children are culpable for their parents' sins and says that "the soul that sins shall die." This principle not only removes the children from culpability for their parents' sin, but it also establishes that each individual must answer to God in full responsibility for sins committed or virtues achieved. This new principle apparently ran into resistance from the people, who were thoroughly raised in a theology of communal guilt and virtue. The Lord responds to their objection with a fuller statement of the principle of individual responsibility:

[19]"When the son has done what is lawful and right, and has been careful to observe all my statutes, he shall surely live. [20]The soul that sins shall die. The son shall not suffer for the iniquity of the father, nor the father suffer for the iniquity of the son; the righteousness of the righteous shall be upon himself, and the wickedness of the wicked shall be upon himself." (Ezekiel 18:19-20)

Past Sins Will Not Be Remembered

Then the Lord asserts the principle that a wicked person can convert from transgression against God and begin to live a righteous life:

[21]"If a wicked man turns away from all his sins which he has committed and keeps all my statutes and does what is lawful and right, he shall surely live; he shall not die. [22]None of the transgressions which he has committed shall be remembered against him; for the righteousness which he has done he shall live." (Ezekiel 18:21-22)

The past sins will not be counted against the wicked person, but he will be rewarded for his newfound righteousness. Underlying this principle is the Lord's rhetorical question: "Have I any pleasure in the death of the wicked, says the Lord GOD, and not rather that he should turn from his way and live?" (Ezekiel 18:23). Therefore, he explicitly states that he wants the wicked to turn away from sin and live.

A corollary to this principle of the conversion of the wicked to righteousness is introduced:

[24]"But when a righteous man turns away from his righteousness and commits iniquity and does the same abominable things that the wicked man does, shall he live? None of the righteous deeds which he has done shall be remembered; for the treachery of which he is guilty and the sin he has committed, he shall die." (Ezekiel 18:24)

So it is also possible for the righteous person to revert into sin and thereby destroy his life. His previous righteousness will not count anymore, and the Lord judges him on the basis of the iniquity and treachery for which he is guilty.

The people object to this principle too. The Lord again asserts that his ways are more just than theirs. Therefore, he summons them to repent and acquire a new heart and spirit so that he need not punish them. God's desire is to save the people and give them life, but this hope is dependent on their turning from transgression in order to live righteously (Ezekiel 18:29-32).

This passage from Ezekiel is a turning point that highlights personal responsibility in Israel's moral thinking after centuries of their paying more attention to corporate responsibility. Certainly, individual responsibility was an earlier component of Israelite mentality, as evidenced, for instance, by the way the Book of Deuteronomy alternates between addressing Israel as "you" plural and "you" singular. This distinction is often lost in English because, unlike Hebrew, it uses one word for both the plural and the singular. However, typically the emphasis was on the responsibility of the whole people and the effects of sin on society's fate.

TAKEAWAY: *We are responsible for our own sins and must answer to God for them.*

In addition to individual responsibility, Ezekiel teaches that God judges people on the current state of their relationship with God, not on the past. The people react negatively because they expect their good and bad deeds to be weighed in a balance, with a cumulative judgment of their deeds. If everything averages out, then the person is "safe" with God. This bases the relationship with God on a businesslike negotiation in which someone can build up enough merit to make up for past misdeeds. However, Ezekiel pictures the final state of one's relationship with God as the ultimate determinant of God's judgment; previous actions do not determine it. Ezekiel understands the relationship with God in very personal terms as requiring full integrity in the quality of the relationship. Therefore, even if the relationship had been good at one point in life, deterioration at a later stage will nullify the whole relationship. A choice to ignore the moral demands that God makes on his people is a sin that interrupts the personal relationship. If that is the state of a soul at the end of life, then the soul is doomed. Only the soul that lives the relationship with moral integrity until the end of life will be able to live on with God.

One way to better understand this is to return to the earlier image of the person as clay and the Lord as the potter. Throughout the span of life, the clay can be molded and shaped. However, at the end of life we can say that the clay is fired in the kiln of death. At that point, the clay takes on its permanent, eternal shape and can no longer be molded. If someone lets God shape him or her into his own image and likeness, then death will preserve that image and likeness of God for all eternity. However, if a person refuses to let God shape him or her, then the final shape will contradict God's image and likeness and will be fired into eternal horror and disgrace. Ezekiel 18 lays the choice before each individual: will your relationship with God be characterized by a moral integrity in which he has shaped you—or not?

TAKEAWAY: *It is our current relationship with God that matters.*

Return to the Lord with Your Whole Heart

A classic passage at the very end of Moses' life as recorded in Deuteronomy is a clear statement of God's judgment on Israel. Interestingly, it is addressed to "you" singular, indicating the responsibility of each individual to accept God's judgment and personally obey God's law. A first point to notice is that the Lord holds out the possibility of conversion even after he has punished Israel through exile:

> [2]"Return to the LORD your God, you and your children, and obey his voice in all that I command you this day, with all your heart and with all your soul; [3]then the LORD your God will restore your fortunes, and have compassion upon you, and he will gather you again from all the peoples where the LORD your God has scattered you." (Deuteronomy 30:2-3)

A second point is that this return to the Lord will entail an interior conversion that the Lord will effect by his own action on their hearts:

> ⁶"And the LORD your God will circumcise your heart and the heart of your offspring, so that you will love the LORD your God with all your heart and with all your soul, that you may live. . . . ⁸And you shall again obey the voice of the LORD, and keep all his commandments which I command you this day. ⁹The LORD your God will make you abundantly prosperous in all the work of your hand, in the fruit of your body, and in the fruit of your cattle, and in the fruit of your ground; for the LORD will again take delight in prospering you, as he took delight in your fathers, ¹⁰if you obey the voice of the LORD your God, to keep his commandments and his statutes which are written in this book of the law, if you turn to the LORD your God with all your heart and with all your soul." (Deuteronomy 30:6, 8-10)

Just as in Ezekiel, where the Lord did not take delight in the death of the sinner but in his life, so here also does the Lord delight in the prosperity of his people. However, the condition for this prosperity is that the converted person obey the Lord, keep his commandments, and turn to him with all his heart and soul. This conversion is not merely an external act but a change of the whole human interior life.

A third point is that God's commandments are neither too difficult to keep nor too remote from the human mind and heart to understand:

> ¹¹"For this commandment which I command you this day is not too hard for you, neither is it far off. ¹²It is not in heaven, that you should say, 'Who will go up for us to heaven, and

bring it to us, that we may hear it and do it?' [13]Neither is it beyond the sea, that you should say, 'Who will go over the sea for us, and bring it to us, that we may hear it and do it?' [14]But the word is very near you; it is in your mouth and in your heart, so that you can do it." (Deuteronomy 30:11-14)

Each person has the capacity to know God's law and keep it; therefore, each person will be responsible for obeying it. Finally, the choice of one's fate is laid out clearly:

[15] "See, I have set before you this day life and good, death and evil. [16]If you obey the commandments of the LORD your God which I command you this day, by loving the LORD your God, by walking in his ways, and by keeping his commandments and his statutes and his ordinances, then you shall live and multiply, and the LORD your God will bless you in the land which you are entering to take possession of it. [17]But if your heart turns away, and you will not hear, but are drawn away to worship other gods and serve them, [18]I declare to you this day, that you shall perish; you shall not live long in the land which you are going over the Jordan to enter and possess. [19]I call heaven and earth to witness against you this day, that I have set before you life and death, blessing and curse; therefore choose life, that you and your descendants may live, [20]loving the LORD your God, obeying his voice, and cleaving to him; for that means life to you and length of days, that you may dwell in the land which the LORD swore to your fathers, to Abraham, to Isaac, and to Jacob, to give them." (Deuteronomy 30:15-20)

As in Ezekiel 18, the choice is between life and death, blessing and curse. In Deuteronomy 30:19-20, God makes it clear that he has his own definite desire for people: choose life, not only for your own sake, but for your descendants as well. This attitude finds continuity in John 3:16: "God so loved the world . . . " On the human side, the choice for life entails loving God, obeying his voice, and cleaving to him—qualities of a personal relationship such as Ezekiel 18 assumes. This appeal to choose life assumes the existence of free will in the individual, and it also means that a person can say no to God and choose death instead.

TAKEAWAY: *The Lord desires that we return to him with our whole heart, but he leaves that decision up to us. We can choose life or death.*

Hold Fast to Christ

As in Ezekiel 18 and Deuteronomy 30, the New Testament assumes that humans can choose between good and evil, faith or unbelief. Jesus' very first proclamation in the Gospel of Mark implies the possibility and need to make a choice for good: "The time is fulfilled, and the kingdom of God is at hand; repent, and believe in the gospel" (1:15). Furthermore, as in Ezekiel 18, a wicked person can convert and become good, while a good person can change and become wicked. This is most clearly taught in Hebrews:

[12]Take care, brethren, lest there be in any of you an evil, unbelieving heart, leading you to fall away from the living God. [13]But exhort one another every day, as long as

it is called "today," that none of you may be hardened by the deceitfulness of sin. [14]For we share in Christ, if only we hold our first confidence firm to the end. (Hebrews 3:12-14)

In the Book of Hebrews, the audience is composed of Christian believers, any one of whom can develop an "evil, unbelieving heart" that can lead them to fall away from God. As in Ezekiel 18, the principle is that we continue to "share in Christ" only on the condition that "we hold our first confidence firm to the end." The relationship with God must be sustained until the end of life, at which point comes the judgment: "It is appointed for men to die once, and after that comes judgment" (Hebrews 9:27). According to Hebrews 10:22, we ought to have a "true heart in full assurance of faith," and by baptism, our bodies are washed and our hearts are cleansed from an evil conscience. This is the state of the authentic Christian. However, there is a warning for Christians to sustain hope, love, good works, and Christian fellowship in the liturgy:

[23]Let us hold fast the confession of our hope without wavering, for he who promised is faithful; [24]and let us consider how to stir up one another to love and good works, [25]not neglecting to meet together, as is the habit of some, but encouraging one another, and all the more as you see the Day drawing near.

[26]For if we sin deliberately after receiving the knowledge of the truth, there no longer remains a sacrifice for sins, [27]but a fearful prospect of judgment, and a fury of fire which will consume the adversaries. [28]A man who has violated the

law of Moses dies without mercy at the testimony of two or three witnesses. [29]How much worse punishment do you think will be deserved by the man who has spurned the Son of God, and profaned the blood of the covenant by which he was sanctified, and outraged the Spirit of grace? [30]For we know him who said, "Vengeance is mine, I will repay." And again, "The Lord will judge his people." [31]It is a fearful thing to fall into the hands of the living God. (Hebrews 10:23-31)

In Hebrews 10:26, we are particularly warned against committing deliberate sin after having received knowledge of the truth. In Hebrews 10:29, this is equated with having "spurned the Son of God, and profaned the blood of the covenant by which he was sanctified, and outraged the Spirit of grace." Though some Christians teach that once a Christian is saved, he is always saved, this passage makes it very clear that a person of faith who has already been sanctified still remains capable of spurning the Son of God and the Holy Spirit, thereby falling under condemnation.

As Ezekiel had made clear in his day, the righteous can fall back into wickedness as easily as the wicked can convert to goodness. Though the Christian can come to believe only because he or she receives the grace of faith from God as an undeserved gift, that gift does not annul the free will to later reject salvation. As in Ezekiel and Deuteronomy, the believer is exhorted to "hold fast the confession of our hope without wavering" (Hebrews 10:23), staying within the relationship of faith, hope, and love until death. The final moment of judgment determines eternal life or condemnation. The way to prepare for that moment, which comes to everyone at an unknown time, is to remain in the relationship with the Father, Son, and Holy Spirit at every moment of life.

[35]Therefore do not throw away your confidence, which has a great reward. [36]For you have need of endurance, so that you may do the will of God and receive what is promised. [37]"For yet a little while, / and the coming one shall come and shall not tarry; / [38]but my righteous one shall live by faith, / and if he shrinks back, / my soul has no pleasure in him." [39]But we are not of those who shrink back and are destroyed, but of those who have faith and keep their souls. (Hebrews 10:35-39)

By exhorting the Christians not to "shrink back," this final exhortation in Hebrews 10 underscores the ability of our free will to throw away our confidence in God. Each Christian needs endurance—the ability to remain faithful until the end of our lives. What's at stake, according to this passage, is the "great reward" of God's promise or the destruction of the soul. As Moses told Israel, choose life and blessing, or death and a curse (Deuteronomy 30:19).

TAKEAWAY: *We need to remain faithful to the end.*

Jesus also addresses this issue in the parable of the two sons and what made them righteous:

[28]"What do you think? A man had two sons; and he went to the first and said, 'Son, go and work in the vineyard today.'

[29]And he answered, 'I will not'; but afterward he repented and went. [30]And he went to the second and said the same; and he answered, 'I go, sir,' but did not go. [31]Which of the two did the will of his father?" They said, "The first." Jesus said to them, "Truly, I say to you, the tax collectors and the harlots go into the kingdom of God before you. [32]For John came to you in the way of righteousness, and you did not believe him, but the tax collectors and the harlots believed him; and even when you saw it, you did not afterward repent and believe him." (Matthew 21:28-32)

Jesus explicitly applied this parable to people who had followed a life of sin—the tax collectors and harlots—yet who repented when they heard the preaching of John the Baptist and, later, of Jesus himself. However, those who were following the law did not believe the good news of repentance that John had preached, and neither did they accept Jesus' preaching. Therefore, they placed themselves in the category of the second son who accepted obedience in words but not in action. They may have choosen words of obedience, but they chose not to do the will of the Father.

We Need an Ongoing Relationship with God

Each of us as individuals can be shaped and molded like clay throughout the whole of our lives. Various forces try to shape us—the world, the evil spirit, and the "flesh" of our passions. However, God the Creator is the only one who knows how to shape human life in his own image and likeness, which is the purpose of every human being. The other forces will distort the image of God in the person and make it ugly. Based on this understanding, both Ezekiel and Hebrews remind believers that they cannot rest on one decision in the past to be judged good and faithful. Rather, each of us has free will to choose at any moment of our lives to remain faithful to God or to turn against him.

Therefore, we are called to understand life as an ongoing relationship with God in which each of us continues to make choices to accept God's graces or reject them, to believe or to give up faith, to have hope in eternal life or to despair, to love or to hate. Following the image of the clay vessel, death is the moment when the clay is fired and can no longer be shaped. We have our eternal shape from that point on. If we have been shaped by the world, the flesh, and the devil, then we are distorted and destined for an eternity in hell. If we have allowed God to form us into his own image and likeness, we can enjoy the glories of heaven for all eternity, glories that flow from the fact of knowing how much God loves us and sharing in that love with every other person in heaven, whether angelic or human.

–Questions for Reflection and Discussion–

1. As the potter, God is continually shaping us into his image. How is he shaping you now? In what current struggles or circumstances in your life do you see his hand molding you into his image?

2. Do you feel free to make choices in your life? Are there circumstances in which you feel more like a "victim" than as a free agent endowed by God with the will to choose between

good and evil? How could a change in attitude and under-standing of the gift of free will help?

3. When God looks at you today, do you think he is seeing your past sins or only where you are at the moment? Why is it comforting to know that God will not base his judgment of you on previous actions for which you have already repented?

4. Why does the author of the Book of Hebrews warn Christians against backsliding? What can we do in our own lives to prevent this from happening?

5. Which of the two sons do you identify with in Jesus' parable (Matthew 21:28-32)? When in your life have you said no, but then did the Father's will? When have you said yes, but failed to do it?

Freedom from the Slavery of Sin

Goal of Chapter 5: *To understand sin as a form of slavery from which Christ has freed us, and to use our freedom to love and serve others.*

Scripture Highlights: *John 8:31-36; Romans 6:12-13, 16-23; Galatians 5:13-15; Titus 3:3-7; 1 Peter 2:16-17*

Slavery—and deliverance from it by the hand of God—is a theme that runs throughout the Old and New Testaments. Israel's experience of enslavement in Egypt and subsequent liberation by the Lord's mighty deeds formed them into a nation. While dwelling in Egypt, the Israelites were forced into slavery, causing a misery that made them cry out to God (Exodus 2:23). The Lord heard their cry and called Moses to free them (3:7-10). Deliverance from slavery became a model for understanding salvation.

The New Testament presents the idea of sin as a form of slavery. In the Gospel of John, Jesus speaks of the freedom that results from following him, in contrast to the enslaving bonds of sin: "If you continue in my word, you are truly my disciples, and you will know the truth, and the truth will make you free" (8:31-32). The faith of these Jews is a starting point from which they are to continue in his word as true disciples. Their faith is not a vague acceptance of Jesus but has the specific content of the word that the Father had given him to speak in the world. The truth of his word is so powerful that it can set people free. However, the idea of freedom is not clear to the listeners, since they say, "We . . . have never been in bondage to any one" (8:33). Then Jesus explains, "Truly, truly, I say to you, every one who commits sin is a slave to sin. The slave does not continue in the house for ever; the son continues for ever. So if the Son makes you free, you will be free indeed" (8:34-36).

One point that Jesus makes is that sin has greater power than the human who commits it. Once a person engages in sinful acts, the sin has control over him or her. Another point is that because of that slavery to sin, the person does not belong to the family— "house" (John 8:35) here does not mean the residence building but is a common term referring to the family. Sin thus separates the person from the status of membership in the family. Then Jesus' point about continuing in his word becomes more significant: it gives the disciple a freedom that equals membership in the family. God is truly Father, and the believer enters into a new relationship with Jesus, the only begotten Son of God.

Later in this Gospel, Jesus will promise an eternal dwelling with the Father and the Son as a way to show the true freedom of belonging to the family: "In my Father's house are many rooms; if it were not so, would I have told you that I go to prepare a place for you? And when I go and prepare a place for you, I will come again and will take you to myself, that where I am you may be also" (John 14:2-3). "If a man loves me, he will keep my word, and my Father will love him, and we will come to him and make our home with him" (14:23). While slavery means being owned and dominated by the power of sin, freedom means eternal belonging and being at home with God, who loves us.

TAKEAWAY: *Sin has the power to enslave us and separates us from the family of God.*

St. Paul's Explanation

St. Paul provides the most complete analysis of sin as slavery and as freedom in Christ, especially in his Letter to the Romans. In chapter 6 of Romans, he explains that in baptism, we enter the death of Jesus so that we can rise with him, putting sin to death in our lives (6:1-11). Then he exhorts baptized Christians to avoid slavery to sin. As we read this passage, keep in mind that the Israelites desired to return to slavery in Egypt after they had crossed the Red Sea (cf. Exodus 14:11-12).

> [12]Let not sin therefore reign in your mortal bodies, to make you obey their passions. [13]Do not yield your members to sin as instruments of wickedness, but yield yourselves to God as men who have been brought from death to life, and your members to God as instruments of righteousness. (Romans 6:12-13)

Paul prepares for the discussion of slavery to sin by explaining that when sin reigns in one's body, passions take control of life. When passion is in charge, then a person does not respond to the choices made by the power of reason. Reason helps us think through the proper strategies and actions of the goals we want to achieve and the way in which we can achieve them. With our passions, we react to immediate impulses and then follow these impulses without consideration of the appropriate purpose or goal of our actions. Therefore, Paul exhorts Christians to "yield [themselves] to God" so as to make the members of the body "instruments of righteousness."

Next, St. Paul lays down a fundamental choice: "Do you not know that if you yield yourselves to any one as obedient slaves, you are slaves of the one whom you obey, either of sin, which leads to death, or of obedience, which leads to righteousness?" (Romans 6:16). He understands that people will necessarily be in some form of servitude, either to sin or to righteousness. He makes clear that sin has eternal consequences in spiritual death, while righteousness results in life. Though he has spoken of a slavery to righteousness, he also speaks of the freedom of ending our slavery to sin:

> [17]But thanks be to God, that you who were once slaves of sin have become obedient from the heart to the standard of teaching to which you were committed, [18]and, having been set free from sin, have become slaves of righteousness. [19]I am speaking in human terms, because of your natural limitations. For just as you once yielded your members to impurity and to greater and greater iniquity, so now yield your members to righteousness for sanctification. (Romans 6:17-19)

Ironically, he identifies slavery to sin as freedom from righteousness. Many people continue to seek freedom from righteousness because they consider the rules of the moral life too constraining. Such people do not think that righteous behavior allows for free self-expression. They identify freedom from righteousness as freedom from society's rules. They do not think about righteousness as a value in itself but merely as a social convention that inhibits them.

> [20]When you were slaves of sin, you were free in regard to righteousness. [21]But then what return did you get from the things of which you are now ashamed? The end of those things is death. [22]But now that you have been set free from sin and have become slaves of God, the return you get is sanctification and its end, eternal life. [23]For the wages of sin is death, but the free gift of God is eternal life in Christ Jesus our Lord. (Romans 6:20-23)

Freedom from sin and slavery to God means holiness and eternal life in Christ Jesus. Following one's passions does not offer hope of eternal life; it is inherently focused on the present moment and nothing more. Commitment to righteousness gives hope. One who is committed to righteousness finds a reason and purpose for living, and life becomes exciting, not because of the gratification of immediate passions, but because of future hopes that lead into eternity.

TAKEAWAY: *We are either slaves to sin or slaves to righteousness. When we are committed to righteousness, we have hope.*

How Do We Use Our Freedom?

Another passage by St. Paul, this time in his Letter to the Galatians, is a summons to avoid spiritual slavery so that one can be free: "For freedom Christ has set us free; stand fast therefore, and do not submit again to a yoke of slavery" (5:1). Paul follows this summons with a polemic against being circumcised, which would bring the Christians into slavery under the law (5:2-12). Then he repeats the call to freedom with an admonition to use this freedom in a way that is compatible with their new Christian life:

> [13]For you were called to freedom, brethren; only do not use your freedom as an opportunity for the flesh, but through love be servants of one another. [14]For the whole law is fulfilled in one word, "You shall love your neighbor as yourself." [15]But if you bite and devour one another take heed that you are not consumed by one another. [16]But I say, walk by the Spirit, and do not gratify the desires of the flesh. (Galatians 5:13-16)

While St. Paul frequently warns against slavery to sin, he also includes the positive call to freedom. However, this freedom is not an "opportunity for the flesh" by which a person confuses authentic freedom with a license to sin. Rather, it is a freedom from the control and enslavement of sin so as to be free to love others for their own sake and not for any motives by which someone uses another person, for example, for personal gain or gratification. A lack of love for the dignity of others will lead a person to "bite and devour" and consume others in order to gratify one's flesh.

This leads a person to spiritual death and greatly harms the people who are being treated as mere objects.

St. Paul commissioned a disciple, Titus, to be the bishop of Crete. Paul wrote one epistle to him to instruct him on how to guide the Christian community. One paragraph in particular describes slavery to sin and the salvation of God.

> [3]For we ourselves were once foolish, disobedient, led astray, slaves to various passions and pleasures, passing our days in malice and envy, hated by men and hating one another; [4]but when the goodness and loving kindness of God our Savior appeared, [5]he saved us, not because of deeds done by us in righteousness, but in virtue of his own mercy, by the washing of regeneration and renewal in the Holy Spirit, [6]which he poured out upon us richly through Jesus Christ our Savior, [7]so that we might be justified by his grace and become heirs in hope of eternal life. (Titus 3:3-7)

God saved us when his "goodness and loving kindness" appeared as antidotes to our slavery to sin. This salvation was not accomplished by us sinners; we were incapable of gaining a righteousness of our own (Titus 3:5). However, his mercy and the "washing of regeneration," that is, baptism, "and renewal in the Holy Spirit . . . poured out . . . through Jesus Christ" justified us by grace. It is good to note the link between the teaching on baptism and freedom from sin, similar to the teaching in Romans 6. We can therefore go forward in hope of eternal life, filled with gratitude for the freedom from slavery that God has accomplished for us in Christ Jesus.

St. Peter makes the same points when he writes: "Live as free men, yet without using your freedom as a pretext for evil; but live as servants of God. Honor all men. Love the brotherhood. Fear God" (1 Peter 2:16-17). He and St. Paul were both aware of the temptation to use freedom as a pretext for the evil of moral license. The freedom to which they call Christians means being a servant of God, specifically by loving all people and honoring God. A servant of God will recognize the dignity God bestows on every human being made in his image and likeness. This honor and love for other people will never become an occasion to use them or abuse them.

TAKEAWAY: *Freedom from sin means freedom to love others for their own sake.*

Understanding sin as a form of slavery can be helpful in our own battle against sin. God wants us to be free, not enslaved to anything. He also wants us to dwell in his house, with his family. When we view sin as robbing us of this freedom, it makes us all the more determined to be true sons or daughters of our heavenly Father. In the next two chapters, we will deal with those things that tempt us to sin—the flesh, the world, and the devil.

–Questions for Reflection and Discussion–

1. Have you ever viewed sin as a form of slavery? Why is that an apt description? In what ways have you experienced sin as being enslaved?

2. How does our society confuse authentic freedom with a license to sin? How is freedom portrayed by St. Paul? What are we free *to do*?

3. How does freedom from sin help us to truly love others? How have you seen this in your own life? Is there a sin you are struggling with now that is preventing you from loving someone authentically?

4. St. Paul instructs us to "be servants of one another" through love (Galatians 5:13). Some would see servants and slaves as one and the same. In Paul's view, how are they different?

5. Jesus described freedom as being at home with God and belonging to his Father's family (John 8:33-36). Slaves are not members of the family, and so they do not belong in the family's house. How can you reach out to those outside of God's family and offer them a home with God? What might you say that would help them to see sin as a form of bondage?

The Battle between the Flesh and the Spirit

Goals of Chapter 6: (1) *To acknowledge that we all struggle with temptations of the flesh.* (2) *To understand that we cannot win this battle on our own; only Christ, through the power of the Holy Spirit, can help us.*

Scripture Highlights: *Romans 7:14-25; 8:1-25; Galatians 5:17-26*

St. Paul had been trained as a Pharisee (Acts 23:6; 26:4-5; Philippians 3:5), which included a strong education in Jewish law. As a Christian apostle, he still held the position that the law is "spiritual" and "good" and says that he delights in it (Roman 7:14, 16, 22). However, in this autobiographical section of his Letter to the Romans (7:14-25), Paul admits that while he wants to obey the law of God, he finds himself unable to do so. He analyzes his personal situation so as to offer theological and spiritual reflections on his problem, thus helping other Christians who struggle with the same difficulty.

St. Paul identifies the problem succinctly: "I am carnal, sold under sin" (Romans 7:14). Being "carnal" translates an adjective derived from the Greek word for "flesh," which is distinct from the "body." The word "flesh" is commonly used to mean that which is corrupt in human nature and can give power to sin. The impact of the flesh is to pull a person away from the true desires of the spirit, so Paul says:

[15]I do not understand my own actions. For I do not do what I want, but I do the very thing I hate. [16]Now if I do what I do not want, I agree that the law is good. [17]So then it is no longer I that do it, but sin which dwells within me. [18]For I know that nothing good dwells within me, that is, in my flesh. I can will what is right, but I cannot do it. [19]For I do not do the good I want, but the evil I do not want is what I do. [20]Now if I do what I do not want, it is no longer I that do it, but sin which dwells within me. [21]So I find it to be a law that when I want to do right, evil lies close at hand. [22]For I delight in the law of God, in my inmost self, [23]but I see in my members another law at war with the law of my mind and making me captive to the law of sin which dwells in my members. (Romans 7:15-23)

Anyone who has tried something as simple as going on a diet can relate to Paul's dilemma. This is profoundly true of those who try to break habits of sin that are embedded in the flesh, such as addictions to alcohol, drugs, sex, gambling, or many other vices. Having faced this weakness of the flesh himself, Paul cries out in what initially appears to be despair: "Wretched man that I am! Who will deliver me from this body of death?" (Romans 7:24). The hope that he finds in this state of his soul is in his faith: "Thanks be to God through Jesus Christ our Lord! So then, I of myself serve the law of God with my mind, but with my flesh I serve the law of sin. There is therefore now no condemnation for those who are in Christ Jesus" (7:25–8:1).

Paul cannot look to himself as a source of hope because he is aware of the interior struggle between trying to do good and the resistance to achieving it. He remains aware of his failure to resolve this struggle in favor of goodness. Yet he is also aware of the gracious forgiveness and reconciliation that God has given him through Jesus Christ (cf. Romans 3:23-28; 5:1-11).

TAKEAWAY: *We all struggle with resisting the temptations and sins of the flesh, and we cannot resolve this dilemma on our own.*

There Is No Condemnation in Christ

In fact, he is so convinced of the free gift of reconciliation that with joy and triumph he proclaims, "There is therefore now no condemnation for those who are in Christ Jesus" (Romans 8:1). This statement of faith stands in contrast to the very frequently stated self-understanding of many contemporaries. "I'm a good person," such people frequently say. They may remark, "I haven't killed anyone" or "I don't steal." Defining one's own goodness on the basis of the sins that one does not commit is hardly a defense. Not only does it ignore the sins that one does commit, but it ignores faith in the only one who has the power to reconcile us with God—Jesus Christ. Christians of every age need to focus on the operative phrase here: "There is . . . no condemnation for those who are in Christ Jesus." Being in Christ determines the state of reconciliation with God; one's self-evaluation as a "good person" does not.

St. Paul continues to describe the content of his faith in Jesus Christ that explains why there is no condemnation:

> [2]For the law of the Spirit of life in Christ Jesus has set me free from the law of sin and death. [3]For God has done what the law, weakened by the flesh, could not do: sending his own Son in the likeness of sinful flesh and for sin, he condemned sin in the flesh, [4]in order that the just requirement of the law might be fulfilled in us, who walk not according to the flesh but according to the Spirit. (Romans 8:2-4)

First, notice that God is the one who has "condemned sin in the flesh" because only he is capable of doing so. The law is "weakened by the flesh" and therefore does not have the power on its own to change Paul's weakness or anyone else's. Second, the means by which God has condemned sin in the flesh is the mission of his own Son. Besides the fact of being God's Son, Jesus is also said to be "in the likeness of sinful flesh." Recall the New Testament pattern of statements from chapter 3 about Christ's divinity being followed by teachings about his death on the cross. Here in Romans 8:3, the power to condemn sin comes from being God the Son "in the likeness of sinful flesh," which is another way of expressing Jesus' emptying of himself of his divinity in order to be born a servant who dies on the cross (cf. Philippians 2:6-11).

TAKEAWAY: *Only in Christ can we experience victory over our struggles with the flesh.*

Walking by the Spirit

As we pointed out in chapter 3, the infinite divinity of Christ and his true humanity make it possible for him to reconcile the sins of human beings with the divine majesty. Only a human could justly make up for human sins, but since the sins have infinite value, only the true God could reconcile the sinners. Therefore, St. Paul mentions the "just requirement of the law" being fulfilled in Christ, allowing us to "walk not according to the flesh but according to the Spirit" (Romans 8:4). Redemption, therefore, entails a new "law of the Spirit of life in Christ Jesus" that sets the Christian "free from the law of sin and death" (8:2). The idea of freedom from sin and death is another aspect of Paul's teaching in Roman 6:12-23, where slavery to sin brings a person death (see chapter 5).

The next passage in Romans clarifies the difference between the flesh and the Spirit:

> [5]For those who live according to the flesh set their minds on the things of the flesh, but those who live according to the Spirit set their minds on the things of the Spirit. [6]To set the mind on the flesh is death, but to set the mind on the Spirit is life and peace. [7]For the mind that is set on the flesh is hostile to God; it does not submit to God's law, indeed it cannot; [8]and those who are in the flesh cannot please God. (Romans 8:5-8)

As the passages highlighted in chapter 4 showed, a radical decision to choose obedience to God and life or to choose disobedience and death is set before each human being. St. Paul explains the decision as being one of the flesh, which means "death," or of the Spirit, which means "life and peace" (Romans 8:6). Choosing to live by the flesh establishes hostility to God, thus making it impossible to please God.

To understand this hostility between God and the flesh, it is useful to examine another letter, Galatians, in which St. Paul more fully explains what he means by the flesh:

> [17]For the desires of the flesh are against the Spirit, and the desires of the Spirit are against the flesh; for these are opposed to each other, to prevent you from doing what you would. [18]But if you are led by the Spirit you are not under the law. [19]Now the works of the flesh are plain: immorality, impurity, licentiousness, [20]idolatry, sorcery, enmity, strife, jealousy, anger, selfishness, dissension, party spirit, [21]envy, drunkenness, carousing, and the like. I warn you, as I warned you before, that those who do such things shall not inherit the kingdom of God. (Galatians 5:17-21)

Many people expect the sexual sins to be listed, since that is a common association with the flesh, and drunkenness and carousing are often closely related to the flesh. But there are also religious elements, such as idolatry and sorcery, which include all the occult arts. Various forms of vices are from the flesh—enmity, strife and anger, jealousy and envy, and selfishness. Another surprise is the more ideological side of the flesh: dissension and "party spirit." The last term translates the Greek word *haeresis*, from which comes the English word "heresy," which is also a work of the flesh.

TAKEAWAY: *We encounter the pull of the flesh in many areas of our lives, and if we live by the flesh, we cannot please God.*

The Spirit Brings Life

The Spirit brings life and peace, as evidenced in St. Paul's list of the fruit of the Spirit:

> [22]But the fruit of the Spirit is love, joy, peace, patience, kindness, goodness, faithfulness, [23]gentleness, self-control; against such there is no law. [24]And those who belong to Christ Jesus have crucified the flesh with its passions and desires. [25]If we live by the Spirit, let us also walk by the Spirit. [26]Let us have no self-conceit, no provoking of one another, no envy of one another. (Galatians 5:22-26)

As he lists the virtues that characterize the life of the Spirit, St. Paul explains that belonging to Christ means a union with him, and even a type of crucifixion of the flesh that controls human life through "passions and desires." As in Romans 8:4, the Christian "walks by the Spirit" and not by the flesh. Let us return to Romans 8 to learn more about the ramifications of walking in the Spirit of Christ rather than by the flesh:

> [9]But you are not in the flesh, you are in the Spirit, if the Spirit of God really dwells in you. Any one who does not have the Spirit of Christ does not belong to him. [10]But if Christ is in you, although your bodies are dead because of sin, your spirits are alive because of righteousness. [11]If the Spirit of him

who raised Jesus from the dead dwells in you, he who raised Christ Jesus from the dead will give life to your mortal bodies also through his Spirit who dwells in you. [12]So then, brethren, we are debtors, not to the flesh, to live according to the flesh—[13]for if you live according to the flesh you will die, but if by the Spirit you put to death the deeds of the body you will live. (Romans 8:9-13)

In this passage, St. Paul clarifies the position of Christians in light of the preceding discussion. His first assumption is that the Spirit of God, who is the same as the Spirit of Christ, dwells within the person. If that is true, then we are not in the flesh but in the Spirit because this state is the action of God in us. On the one hand, there is a sense in which the body is dead because of sin; on the other hand, the human spirit lives because of righteousness. Here "righteousness" refers to a presence of moral right that summarizes the more extended list of virtues that are the fruit of the Spirit in Galatians 5:22-23. The Spirit is identified here as "the Spirit of him who raised Jesus from the dead." Because this Spirit dwells within the Christian, God, who raised Jesus from the dead, is able to give life even to our mortal bodies, showing that he is so much stronger than the power of sin that brings death.

From these statements of faith, Paul concludes that we are not debtors to the flesh by which we live according to the flesh, with death as the sole prospect. Instead, Christians live by the Spirit and put to death the works of the flesh. This promises life.

TAKEAWAY: *The Spirit dwells in us, giving us life. He is much stronger than the power of sin that brings death.*

The next section of Romans contains important links to Jesus' teaching about slavery to sin in John 8:34-36.

> [14]For all who are led by the Spirit of God are sons of God. [15]For you did not receive the spirit of slavery to fall back into fear, but you have received the spirit of sonship. When we cry, "Abba! Father!" [16]it is the Spirit himself bearing witness with our spirit that we are children of God, [17]and if children, then heirs, heirs of God and fellow heirs with Christ, provided we suffer with him in order that we may also be glorified with him. (Romans 8:14-17)

Here St. Paul emphasizes the role of the Holy Spirit in the life of the Christian. He makes a contrast between the "spirit of slavery" that makes a person "fall back into fear" and the role of the Holy Spirit within the human spirit in bestowing a filial relationship with God. Just as in 1 Corinthians 12:3, when St. Paul says that "no one can say 'Jesus is Lord' except by the Holy Spirit," so too here the Holy Spirit is necessary to enable one to cry out, "Abba! Father!" Though this translation uses the term "spirit of sonship," the more accurate translation of the Greek is "adoption." This is important because adoption distinguishes the unique sonship of Jesus, the Word-made-flesh and only begotten Son (John 1:14), from the adoption of us sinners into the family. By this adoption, Jesus is our brother and God is our Father. This filial relationship also means that we are coheirs of the glory of God, so long as we share in Christ's sufferings.

The Hope of All Creation

In the last passage that we will discuss from Romans 8, St. Paul highlights the effects of the life of the Spirit within Christians on the creation as a whole:

> [18]I consider that the sufferings of this present time are not worth comparing with the glory that is to be revealed to us. [19]For the creation waits with eager longing for the revealing of the sons of God; [20]for the creation was subjected to futility, not of its own will but by the will of him who subjected it in hope; [21]because the creation itself will be set free from its bondage to decay and obtain the glorious liberty of the children of God. [22]We know that the whole creation has been groaning in travail together until now; [23]and not only the creation, but we ourselves, who have the first fruits of the Spirit, groan inwardly as we wait for adoption as sons, the redemption of our bodies. [24]For in this hope we were saved. Now hope that is seen is not hope. For who hopes for what he sees? [25]But if we hope for what we do not see, we wait for it with patience. (Romans 8:18-25)

St. Paul changes perspective from the Christian believers to that of creation, which is eagerly expecting the revelation of the children of God that Paul described in the preceding verses. Creation is "subjected to futility" because human sinfulness and the life of the flesh affect creation. One need only consider the effects of industrialization on the rest of creation to be convinced of the truth of Paul's point. However, there is still a component of hope that creation will be freed from corruption and "obtain the glorious liberty of the children of God."

TAKEAWAY: *Because the Spirit dwells in us, we are adopted sons and daughters of God. Therefore, have hope in both the redemption of our bodies and of creation itself.*

St. Paul highlights the hope of freedom that lies in store for Christians and for the whole creation that will be glorified after the general resurrection of the dead at the end of time. Though both creation and Christians might groan during the present condition of the sinful world and the flesh, "we wait for adoption as sons, the redemption of our bodies." We can move forward in life with its great difficulties and personal failures because "in this hope we were saved."

–Questions for Reflection and Discussion–

1. How often do you look to yourself rather than to God in your interior battle with your flesh? Why do you think St. Paul found the answer to this battle in Jesus?

2. Do you see yourself as a "good" person? What is your evaluation based on? On what basis should you evaluate your goodness?

3. What is the difference between a life of the flesh and a life of the Spirit, according to St. Paul? Does anything on his list of "works of the flesh" in Galatians 5:19-20 surprise you because it is included there? Which one do you most struggle with?

4. Do you believe that Jesus living in you is stronger than the power of sin? What could you do to bolster your faith in that regard? How would prayer and meditation on Scripture help?

5. Why does hope play such an important role in our lives as Christians? How has it helped you in your struggle with sin and other personal difficulties?

The Influences of the World and the Devil

Goals of Chapter 7: (1) *To develop a proper perspective of the world, seeing it as God's creation and an object of his love, but also to be aware of the darkness in the world because of sin. Like Jesus, we are called to be a light to the world but we can expect opposition.* (2) *To understand that we must also be on guard against the lies of Satan.*

Scripture Highlights: *John 1:29-30; 3:16-20; 8:12, 23-27; 12:46-48; 14:27; 17:13-19; 2 Corinthians 11:13-14; 2 Timothy 2:24-26*

Traditional theology recognizes a number of influences on the moral decisions everyone makes. The one saving influence is God. Three other influences tend to lead a person to temptation and sin: the devil, the flesh, and the world. The last chapter dealt with the battle between flesh and spirit. In this chapter we will talk about the biblical view of the world and its influence, both good and evil, on us. Then we will talk about how Satan can influence us by leading us to believe falsehoods. The more aware we are of these influences, the more we can win the battle against sin in our lives.

The World in the Gospel of John

In the New Testament, the term "world" has a number of different senses, particularly in the writings of St. John, and so first we will explore these various meanings in his Gospel. We will explore the richness of Christ's teaching on the world so that it may inform our prayer and reflection on our approach to the contemporary world.

The first meaning of "world" refers to creation, the orderly cosmos created as something good at every step of its formation according to Genesis. This meaning underlies John 1:9-10: "The true light that enlightens every man was coming into the world. He was in the world, and the world was made through him, yet the world knew him not." When Jesus refers to the creation of the world as a marker in time, he means the physical cosmos: "Father, glorify me in your own presence with the glory which I had with you before the world was made" (17:5). He prayed to the Father that the disciples might "behold my glory which you have given me in your love for me before the foundation of the world" (17:24).

Compare this understanding of "world" to John 3:31: "He who comes from above is above all; he who is of the earth belongs to the earth, and of the earth he speaks; he who comes from heaven is above all." "Earth" simply refers to the natural world in a morally neutral sense, as does "world" in the texts above. This sense is also used in John's first epistle: "In this is love perfected with us, that we may have confidence for the day of judgment, because as he is so are we in this world" (1 John 4:17). The world is simply the location where the Christian community dwells.

The term "world" takes on greater significance in most of the rest of John's writings. "World" can refer to the inhabited regions where human beings dwell and create their societies, as in the Hebrew word for "world" (*tebel*). With this meaning, the world is the object of God's loving desire to bring salvation and eternal life. One example of God's positive attitude to the world is expressed in the statement by John the Baptist, who saw Jesus and said, "Behold, the Lamb of God, who takes away the sin of the world! This is he of whom I said, 'After me comes a man who ranks before me, for he was before me'" (John 1:29-30). Notice that Jesus is identified by John as the "Lamb of God" who cares so much about the world that he is sent to take away its sins and that Jesus preexists John the Baptist, even as he preexists the world whose sins he will remove.

Another passage proclaims God's amazing love for the world:

[16]For God so loved the world that he gave his only Son, that whoever believes in him should not perish but have eternal life. [17]For God sent the Son into the world, not to condemn the world, but that the world might be saved through him. [18]He who believes in him is not condemned; he who does not believe is condemned already, because he has not believed in the name of the only Son of God. (John 3:16-18)

The fact that God loves the world so much that he gave it his only Son, who is himself God, proves that the love is as infinite as the gift. Verse 17 further emphasizes that God's purpose is to save the world, not condemn it. However, the determining issue is whether the people in the world will have faith in the Son:

faith in the Son means salvation and eternal life, while a refusal to believe means condemnation. These verses announce a confidence in God's love for the world, but they also acknowledge the possibility that the world will reject Christ, which is also recognized in the verses that follow:

> [19]And this is the judgment, that the light has come into the world, and men loved darkness rather than light, because their deeds were evil. [20]For every one who does evil hates the light, and does not come to the light, lest his deeds should be exposed. (John 3:19-20)

The very reason for which the Son came into the world was to save it from sin, that is, to be the Lamb who takes away the sin of the world (John 1:29). However, the reality of sin in the world prevents its inhabitants from believing in the Son because he will necessarily shine light on their sins in order to make expiation and bring forgiveness. People fear such exposure.

TAKEAWAY: *The world is the object of God's loving desire. He created it, and his purpose in sending his Son into the world was to save the world, not condemn it.*

Jesus, the Light of the World

In three passages, Jesus announces to his hearers that he has come as a positive light in the world. In the first passage, Jesus says, "I am the light of the world; he who follows me will not walk in darkness, but will have the light of life" (John 8:12). On the one hand, the follower "will not walk in darkness," which implies that darkness is in the world, as does John 1:5: "The light shines in the darkness, and the darkness has not overcome it." On the other hand, the light will bring life (as was promised in 3:16 and 6:33, 51). In the second passage, Jesus says, "As long as I am in the world, I am the light of the world" (9:5). Obviously, Jesus desires to bring light into the world itself. In the third passage, Jesus says:

> [46]"I have come as light into the world, that whoever believes in me may not remain in darkness. [47]If any one hears my sayings and does not keep them, I do not judge him; for I did not come to judge the world but to save the world. [48]He who rejects me and does not receive my sayings has a judge; the word that I have spoken will be his judge on the last day." (John 12:46-48)

While Jesus is truly the light of the world, people in the world still need to have faith in him in order to move out of the darkness and into the light. Hearing and keeping Jesus' word is required, along with faith, in order to avoid condemnation and receive salvation. These saving words were given to Jesus by the Father, who sent him into the world, and therefore they give eternal life, as do belief in him (John 3:16) and the eating of his flesh (6:51). Christ's statements about being light in the world all indicate his loving mission to the world.

One long section in John's Gospel (chapters 7–8) portrays antagonism toward Jesus during the feast of Tabernacles (7:2). Before he leaves Galilee, his brothers urge him to go to Judea so that he can show himself "to the world" (7:3-4), but the

Evangelist notes that they say this because "even his brethen did not believe in him" (7:5). Jesus' response to their lack of faith is harsh: "My time has not yet come, but your time is always here. The world cannot hate you, but it hates me because I testify of it that its works are evil" (7:6-7). He indicates that these brothers without faith are still in the darkness of evil deeds, and the world finds them to be no threat to its own evil. Even though Jesus has been sent into the world to save it and give it eternal life, he does not hesitate to testify that its works are evil.

While this discourse includes Jesus' first assertion that he is the light of the world (John 8:12), nonetheless, he makes a strong criticism of the world and his relationship with it:

> [23]"You are from below, I am from above; you are of this world, I am not of this world. [24]I told you that you would die in your sins, for you will die in your sins unless you believe that I am he." [25]They said to him, "Who are you?" Jesus said to them, "Even what I have told you from the beginning. [26]I have much to say about you and much to judge; but he who sent me is true, and I declare to the world what I have heard from him." [27]They did not understand that he spoke to them of the Father. (John 8:23-27)

Jesus contrasts his origins with those of his audience: he is "from above" and "not of this world," while they are "from below" and "of this world." This is consistent with all the passages that say he is from the Father and was sent into the world to save it. His next point is that he has been sent to save them from their sins. Sin is what keeps the world in darkness, while the one way out of sin is to believe that Jesus is "I am." Here Jesus is claiming to be "I am," the name God gives himself in Exodus 3:14. Later in this chapter, Jesus will again make this claim, adding to it his preexistence of Abraham: "Truly, truly, I say to you, before Abraham was, I am" (John 8:58). Belief in Jesus' divinity is the key to becoming free of the sin that characterizes belonging to the world. However, the end result of this episode is that "they took up stones to throw at him; but Jesus hid himself, and went out of the temple" (8:59). That crowd did not come to believe in him or receive salvation from him.

TAKEAWAY: *The world is in darkness because of sin, but Jesus is the light of the world. The way out of this darkness is to believe in him.*

Christ, Not the World, Gives Us Peace

In his Last Supper discourse, Jesus presents another contrast between himself and the world: "Peace I leave with you; my peace I give to you; not as the world gives do I give to you. Let not your hearts be troubled, neither let them be afraid" (John 14:27). The peace that Jesus gives will last into eternal life, which is the purpose of his coming into the world. His peace brings integrity to the person, establishing a wholeness within the individual, as well as within the community and its inner relationships. An amazing aspect of the experience of Christian peace is that a person can reach the point of admitting sin and wrongdoing, accompanied by feelings of guilt, yet Christ can bring peace into that situation by revealing his forgiveness of the sin. Another awe-inspiring experience of Christ's peace belongs to many Christians over the

WINNING THE BATTLE AGAINST SIN

centuries during times of hardship, oppression, and persecution. Despite the losses suffered or the dangers faced, these Christians experience a peace that sustains them through their difficulties. The world is incapable of giving this kind of peace.

As Jesus had already stated, the ruler of the world is the evil spirit (John 12:31). Now in his final words to the apostles, he says, "I will no longer talk much with you, for the ruler of this world is coming" (14:30a). This may be a reference to the fact that earlier, Satan had entered into Judas Iscariot (13:27). Not many hours after this discourse, Judas would betray Jesus in Gethsemane. At that moment, it would seem that the ruler of this world had all the power, as events would become bitter and painful for Jesus. However, Jesus asserts that, contrary to the appearances of his passion and death, the ruler of this world "has no power over me; but I do as the Father has commanded me, so that the world may know that I love the Father" (14:30b-31).

The Disciples' Mission to the World

Having finished the discourse with his disciples (John 13–16), Jesus then "lifted up his eyes to heaven" (17:1) and began a long prayer to his Father. At one point, Jesus compared his mission to the world with the disciples' mission:

> [13]"But now I am coming to you; and these things I speak in the world, that they may have my joy fulfilled in themselves. [14]I have given them your word; and the world has hated them because they are not of the world, even as I am not of the world. [15]I do not pray that you should take them out of the world, but that you should keep them from the evil one.

> [16]They are not of the world, even as I am not of the world. [17]Sanctify them in the truth; your word is truth. [18]As you sent me into the world, so I have sent them into the world. [19]And for their sake I consecrate myself, that they also may be consecrated in truth." (John 17:13-19)

Jesus has given the Father's word to the disciples, letting them in on God's plan to save the world through him. This is the key to his joy. However, this means that they are taken from the world, and therefore its hate and hostility are directed at them. Nevertheless, that does not mean that the Father should remove them from the world; bearing its hatred will be part of their lives, just as it was for Jesus. He simply asks the Father to "keep them from the evil one," who is the world's ruler. This prayer echoes the petition in the Lord's prayer: "And lead us not into temptation, / But deliver us from evil" (Matthew 6:13; cf. Luke 11:4).

Finally, in John 17:17, Jesus prays that the Father "sanctify" the disciples, that is, make them holy in the word of his truth. In 17:19, the same Greek word meaning "sanctify" is translated as "consecrate"; Jesus asks this for himself so that his disciples may also be sanctified in truth. These verses bookend 17:18, as if to say that the mission of the disciples in the world requires them to be sanctified in the truth. Since the world's ruler is the evil one, earlier identified by Jesus as "a liar and the father of lies" (8:44), it will be necessary for Jesus' disciples to be consecrated in truth as an antidote to the falsehoods that permeate the domain of the world.

TAKEAWAY: *The disciples of Jesus are not of the world but are sent into the world with the truth of God's word.*

Developing a Proper Perspective on the World

This overview of the different sense of the "world" in St. John's writings is an important guide for assessing our attitudes toward the world. We can take a positive view of the world as the creation in its entirety and as the location of human habitation. God created the world as good; a sense of wonder at its magnificence is a theme of prayer in Psalms 8 and 104 and is proper to every human being.

We can also grow in a sense of wonder that "God so loved the world" (John 3:16) that he sent his Son to be the Lamb who takes away the sins of the world. We should hear with great joy and expectation Jesus' many promises to bring eternal life to the world and to be its light.

However, even these promises of salvation for the world already contain statements that sin and darkness are in the world. We can see developing more clearly a hostility between Jesus and the world precisely as he proclaimed the good news of salvation and proved his authority by performing miraculous healings. The world's opposition culminated in Jesus' suffering and death, but even before that event, he hammered home several teachings about the world's rejection of the Father, the Son, and the Spirit of truth. That rejection would be the basis of the world's rejection of authentic disciples precisely because they loved the Father and Son and received the Spirit of truth.

At various times of peace in the world, some Christians are tempted to become naïve about the world's fierce opposition to God and the gospel. As a seminarian in the 1960s, I accepted the commonly held optimistic attitude toward the forces working in the world at that time. I believed that the Church, and I, needed to relate better to the culture, accept its premises, and trust that society was evolving in a positive way. The Church could accommodate modern trends and then bring many more people into the community of faith because we would be willing to compromise elements of the gospel. This approach did not pan out well.

When I worked with street gangs in Chicago, I hung out with them to demonstrate that the Church could relate to their world. But I spent so much time learning their ways that I did not teach them much about Christ, the sacraments, the commandments, or anything else. As a college student, I hung out with students and instructors from my favorite class; however, they convinced me that astrology was good, and I learned how to cast horoscopes from them rather than teaching them the gospel. Not only in my life, but in many other circumstances, I witnessed the power of the world to mute the message of Jesus Christ and his gospel as Catholic retreat houses and schools presented New Age ideas or professors taught a Marxist analysis of global economics and politics as a new theological method.

Meanwhile, the culture began turning on the Church. For example, whereas at one time the film industry had been very respectful of the Bible, religion, and the Catholic Church (Catholic-themed movies won Oscars—*Going My Way*, *Song of Bernadette*, and others), in the 1960s and 70s many movies began to mock religion. Today many movies have themes that are anti-religious, especially targeting the Catholic Church.

We can see this cultural aggression against God, Christ, and the Church in the perspective of Jesus' teaching of the world and its opposition to him and to believers. We need not see this as a signal of the end of the world, as some Christians do, but take it as the normal response of a world that rejects and sometimes viciously hates Jesus and us. We need to analyze the darkness that exists in the world so that we can bring the light of Jesus Christ into the darkness. We need to recognize the lies and falsehoods of the world and introduce the Truth who is Christ. We need to see that God still loves the world and continues to send his Son to save those who believe in him; he is still the Lamb of God who takes away the sins of the world, and he is the bread of life who offers eternal life to those who eat his flesh and drink his blood. Christ's rich teaching on the world will give us a proper perspective on the world in which we live and to which we are sent out to bring all people into the unity of the Father, Son, and Holy Spirit. We accept this challenge in the full confidence that Jesus has conquered the world and has defeated the prince of this world through the seeming weakness of his death and the glory of his resurrection. So will he use us in our own weakness to accomplish his powerful redemption.

TAKEAWAY: *While we should take a positive view of the world, we should also know that the world will oppose Jesus and those he sends into the world. As followers of Jesus, we are called to bring the light of Jesus Christ into the darkness.*

The Lies of Satan

Another influence on us already discussed in this chapter is from the evil spirit who is the ruler of the world. Some people fall prey to a variety of demonic temptations, including the attempt to have direct contact with the demonic spirits through occult practices. Other forms of this demonic influence come from rebellion against God, such as Satan's own rebellion against him. Such rebellion usually includes various forms of hatred, such as that manifested by various nationalistic movements like the Nazis or the Japanese empire of the 1930s through 1945, or atheistic governments such as the former Soviet Union, China, or Cambodia. Hundreds of millions of people were killed at the orders of their own government leaders, all of whom are considered monsters in the public mind. These extreme but real examples demonstrate the monstrous influence of the evil spirit, and concentration camps and gulags form its landscape.

St. Paul warned the early Christians about men who were "false apostles," who came to Corinth claiming to have apostolic authority: "For such men are false apostles, deceitful workmen, disguising themselves as apostles of Christ. And no wonder, for even Satan disguises himself as an angel of light" (2 Corinthians 11:13-14). He warns that these men disguise themselves as apostles of Christ, but they follow a pattern observed in Satan, who disguises himself as an angel of light. This is a very important warning about the ability of something evil to transform itself into something that looks good. Rarely does a sinful act show its full evil impact at the beginning of its appearance. We saw in chapter 1 that even after the evil one reminded the woman of God's one commandment, he then proceeded to tempt her to disobedience with the attractive side of evil (Genesis 3:2-6). So also should each person expect that sin will be portrayed as a relatively innocent pleasure or even something useful compared to the guilt one may experience.

A very common temptation from false apostles throughout the centuries is that they will portray heresy and false moral teaching with a variety of enticements. They will describe it as being more reasonable than orthodoxy because it denies some difficult or paradoxical element of the truth. For example, Jehovah's Witnesses deny the divinity of Christ because the Trinitarian doctrine of three Persons in one God does not comply with their logic. Such a simplification makes the heresy more comprehensible, but it does so at the expense of a component of the revelation of God's mystery and therefore of the truth that makes us free (John 8:32). False teaching can also be attractive when it is more in keeping with modern thinking, while the orthodox teaching can seem backward, out-of-date, or even oppressive. This kind of argument is frequently employed to deny various moral teachings, particularly in the sexual realm. Therefore, Christians need to always remain alert to the temptations set out by false apostles and teachers. They can best accomplish this by knowing the fullness of the truths of the Christian faith so that they can use them as the standard by which to judge the teachings of any teacher or group that may cross their paths.

TAKEAWAY: *Knowing the truths of our faith will help us see through the lies of Satan.*

St. Paul wrote two epistles to his disciple Timothy, whom he had left in Ephesus as the bishop to continue teaching the Christian community there. A passage in St. Paul's Second Letter to Timothy deals with the care that Timothy needed to have in order to guard his flock from falsehood:

> [24]And the Lord's servant must not be quarrelsome but kindly to every one, an apt teacher, forbearing, [25]correcting his opponents with gentleness. God may perhaps grant that they will repent and come to know the truth, [26]and they may escape from the snare of the devil, after being captured by him to do his will. (2 Timothy 2:24-26)

The goal St. Paul sets for a bishop is to help opponents to repent, "know the truth," and "escape from the snare of the devil." This goal implies that by not holding to the truth, they are ensnared by the devil, much as Jesus taught when he said that committing sin enslaves one to sin (John 8:34) and when he called Satan "a liar and the father of lies" (8:44). So here in this Second Letter to Timothy, Paul speaks of those who have been ensnared by Satan and do not know the truth; in this captivity Satan gets them to do his will. These opponents of the truth need to repent in order to find Christian freedom. Paul urges Timothy to be kindly, forbearing, and gentle, and thereby be an "apt teacher." Timothy needs the fruit of the Spirit in order to become the kind of teacher that can win those who are captives of Satan through their acceptance of falsehood.

Now let us look to how we can combat the influences of the world, the flesh, and the devil in our lives. The reality is that it is only through Christ that we can we win the victory over sin because he put sin to death on the cross. Let's reflect on that truth in the next chapter.

−Questions for Reflection and Discussion−

1. Where do you see goodness in the world? Where do you see darkness? How does this affect your day-to-day life?

2. Our heavenly Father sent his Son into the world to save it, not to condemn it (John 3:17). What is your relationship with your heavenly Father like? Do you see him as loving the world and ardently desiring all to be saved? Are you ever tempted to believe in a "gotcha" god who is looking to condemn you and others? If so, how can you change your thinking?

3. Have you ever experienced, in the midst of a difficult situation, peace that you knew came from Jesus? Have you ever felt peaceful after going to Confession? How can you seek more of Jesus' peace in your life?

4. Why should Jesus' disciples, then and now, expect opposition and hatred from the world? Have you ever experienced this? How did you respond?

5. How does Satan make evil look attractive? How can you be on guard against the lies of Satan?

PUTTING SIN TO DEATH:
TRANSFORMATION IN CHRIST

Goals of Chapter 8: (1) *To understand the need to put sin to death in our lives so that we can be transformed in Christ.* (2) *To understand the call to be generous in forgiving others.*

Scripture Highlights: *Colossians 3:5-14; 2 Corinthians 4:6-7; 5:17-19; Ephesians 2:13-16; 4:17-24, 31-32; Romans 6:1-12; Matthew 6:9-13*

St. Paul radically changed his life from being a persecutor of Christians who approved of their death to becoming an apostle of Christ who willingly died for his faith. (You can read about his conversion in Acts 9 and Galatians 1:13-24.) He was well aware that people can change their lives by the power of the grace that flows through Christ Jesus, and he often wrote about various aspects of this transformation to encourage and enlighten others about God's ability to shape human lives. In this chapter, we will examine those writings so that we can better understand what Jesus did for us and how we, too, can be transformed in Christ.

St. Paul's baptism was a dramatic episode during which a disciple in Damascus named Ananias reluctantly came to Saul the persecutor, laid hands on him, and said,

> [17]"Brother Saul, the Lord Jesus who appeared to you on the road by which you came, has sent me that you may regain your sight and be filled with the Holy Spirit." [18]And immediately something like scales fell from his eyes and he regained his sight. Then he rose and was baptized. (Acts 9:17-18)

Saul, later using the Greek name Paul, realized the power of baptism and wrote about it many times. In Galatians he introduced a particular image: "For as many of you as were baptized into Christ have put on Christ. There is neither Jew nor Greek, there is neither slave nor free, there is neither male nor female; for you are all one in Christ Jesus" (3:27-28). Among the effects of baptism is the gift of putting on Christ, taking him as the image through which God the Father perceives us.

Putting Sin to Death

The process of transformation into the image of God that Jesus Christ reveals is described as putting sinful actions to death:

> [5]Put to death therefore what is earthly in you: immorality, impurity, passion, evil desire, and covetousness, which is idolatry. [6]On account of these the wrath of God is coming. [7]In these you once walked, when you lived in them. [8]But now put them all away: anger, wrath, malice, slander, and foul talk from your mouth. [9]Do not lie to one another,

seeing that you have put off the old nature with its practices [10]and have put on the new nature, which is being renewed in knowledge after the image of its creator. [11]Here there cannot be Greek and Jew, circumcised and uncircumcised, barbarian, Scythian, slave, free man, but Christ is all, and in all.

[12]Put on then, as God's chosen ones, holy and beloved, compassion, kindness, lowliness, meekness, and patience, [13]forbearing one another and, if one has a complaint against another, forgiving each other; as the Lord has forgiven you, so you also must forgive. [14]And above all these put on love, which binds everything together in perfect harmony. (Colossians 3:5-14)

Note that this passage clearly names a number of sins; it covers a variety of strong feelings or passions such as lust, anger, and wrath, plus specific sins such as fornication, coveting, slander, foul talk, and lies. These are the distortions of the authentic human person that belong to the "old nature" (the Greek word means "old humanity").

St. Paul also implies that we are so attached to the sins of the "old humanity" that we identify ourselves with them. The sins become a pattern of behavior by which other people recognize and accept us, making it even more difficult for us to change. Therefore, he instructs us not to merely retrain the old self but to put it to death so that a new self of virtue, especially of forgiveness and love, can replace the old. This fits Jeremiah's image of God the potter: "And the vessel he was making of clay was spoiled in the potter's hand, and he reworked it into another vessel, as it seemed good to the potter to do" (18:4).

We can use this passage from Colossians as an examination of conscience by which we evaluate the shape of our character and its conformity to Jesus Christ as the norm of life. We can ask ourselves whether the specific sins and passions of the "old self" are still present. When we detect them, we can reject them, confess these sins, and ask Christ to reshape us into his virtues. We can also evaluate ourselves by these specific virtues—compassion, kindness, lowliness, meekness, patience, forbearance, forgiveness, and especially love.

TAKEAWAY: *We are called to put to death the sins that are part of our "old self" and to put on the virtues that conform to Christ.*

A New Creation in Christ

Another way St. Paul speaks of Christian transformation is in terms of a new creation. He first mentions it in his Second Letter to the Corinthians:

> [17]Therefore, if any one is in Christ, he is a new creation; the old has passed away, behold, the new has come. [18]All this is from God, who through Christ reconciled us to himself and gave us the ministry of reconciliation; [19]that is, in Christ God was reconciling the world to himself, not counting their trespasses against them, and entrusting to us the message of reconciliation. (2 Corinthians 5:17-19)

With his own experience in mind, St. Paul understands this new creation as the work of God through Christ. Christ effects this transformation by reconciling us to God through the forgiveness of sins. The Old Testament image of God as the potter is an important reminder that we are all absolutely dependent on the action of God's grace to reshape us into his image and likeness. At the same time, we need to see that being shaped in God's image and likeness is so radical a change in holiness and virtue that St. Paul must describe it as a "new creation."

In his Letter to the Ephesians, St. Paul again describes the process of making a "new man" in terms of a creation that occurs because of Christ's action of reconciling sinners:

> [13]But now in Christ Jesus you who once were far off have been brought near in the blood of Christ. [14]For he is our peace, who has made us both one, and has broken down the dividing wall of hostility, [15]by abolishing in his flesh the law of commandments and ordinances, that he might create in himself one new man in place of the two, so making peace, [16]and might reconcile us both to God in one body through the cross, thereby bringing the hostility to an end. (Ephesians 2:13-16)

The blood of Christ Jesus brings us near to God and to one another. Our proximity to God allows him to reshape us, while sin keeps us too distant from God for Jesus to renew us. Another part of this reconciliation is that Christ's forgiveness extends both to Jews and Gentiles, making them one new people. Therefore, God's new creation through Christ Jesus' saving death on the cross not only transforms individuals but makes a new people. Reconciliation in Christ creates new individuals and a new Israel, the Church formed of Jews and Gentiles.

Again St. Paul describes the contrast between the old and new natures (keep in mind, as noted previously, that the Greek reads "old" and "new humanity"):

> [17]Now this I affirm and testify in the Lord, that you must no longer live as the Gentiles do, in the futility of their minds; [18]they are darkened in their understanding, alienated from the life of God because of the ignorance that is in them, due to their hardness of heart; [19]they have become callous and have given themselves up to licentiousness, greedy to practice every kind of uncleanness. [20]You did not so learn Christ!—[21]assuming that you have heard about him and were taught in him, as the truth is in Jesus. [22]Put off your old nature which belongs to your former manner of life and is corrupt through deceitful lusts, [23]and be renewed in the spirit of your minds, [24]and put on the new nature, created after the likeness of God in true righteousness and holiness. (Ephesians 4:17-24)

St. Paul first calls the Ephesians to reject their former Gentile behavior as the result of the "futility of their minds" that are "darkened in their understanding" and "alienated from the life of God." Their ignorance comes from a "hardness of heart" and callousness, indicating that they are morally culpable for their ignorance. This moral culpability then produces "licentiousness," a term that also means "debauchery" and "sensuality," thereby explaining the "uncleanness" as a reference to sexual sin. Such behavior, typical of their Gentile world, provides a stark contrast to Christ and his truth. Then Paul stresses that it is possible to put on the "new humanity" that is created in the "likeness of God." Its righteous-ness and holiness are true characteristics of the likeness of God. However, by using the word "created" to describe the new human-ity, St. Paul is again highlighting that this process of transformation into God's likeness is itself an action of his grace. Without God accomplishing it, the transformation cannot take place.

TAKEAWAY: *It is God's action in us, through the Holy Spirit, that transforms us into the likeness of God's glory. We can-not accomplish this transformation ourselves.*

St. Paul understands that the transformation of the human per-son into the image and likeness of God is a gift that flows from being able to behold his glory: "And we all, with unveiled face, beholding the glory of the Lord, are being changed into his like-ness from one degree of glory to another; for this comes from the Lord who is the Spirit" (2 Corinthians 3:18). This idea of "beholding the glory of the Lord" indicates that the believer is in a personal relationship with the Lord. This relationship is trans-formative, changing the person by degrees into the glory of God. The weak human being cannot accomplish this transformation alone; the Person of the Holy Spirit is directly operative, shaping the person into the likeness of God's glory.

Then St. Paul returns to the beginning of creation to point out that though we human beings are merely earthly vessels, God has placed an infinite treasure within us:

⁶For it is the God who said, "Let light shine out of dark-ness," who has shone in our hearts to give the light of

the knowledge of the glory of God in the face of Christ. [7]But we have this treasure in earthen vessels, to show that the transcendent power belongs to God and not to us. (2 Corinthians 4:6-7)

The ultimate light that shines in the darkness is "the knowledge of the glory of God in the face of Christ." As St. Paul had said earlier in this letter in verse 3:18, this light is a knowledge that draws the believer into a personal relationship with God and transforms the person. This power of transformation is far superior to the power of the human mind and will alone; it belongs to God, who is actually accomplishing the transformation of clay human vessels into God's image and likeness.

The ultimate result of this process of transformation is immortality: "For this perishable nature must put on the imperishable, and this mortal nature must put on immortality" (1 Corinthians 15:53). God's victory is the transformation of human beings into his image and likeness for all eternity so that we can rejoice as Paul does: "'O death, where is thy victory? / O death, where is thy sting?' The sting of death is sin, and the power of sin is the law. But thanks be to God, who gives us the victory through our Lord Jesus Christ" (15:55-57).

Participating in Christ's Death and Resurrection

In his Letter to the Romans, St. Paul introduces a theology of participation in the process of Christ's death and resurrection. Noting that everyone sins because of the fall of Adam (5:12-17), St. Paul then boldly proclaims, "Where sin increased, grace abounded all the more, so that, as sin reigned in death, grace also might reign through righteousness to eternal life through Jesus Christ our Lord" (5:20-21). However, he rhetorically asks, "Are we to continue in sin that grace may abound? By no means!" (6:1-2). He then explains:

> [2]How can we who died to sin still live in it? [3]Do you not know that all of us who have been baptized into Christ Jesus were baptized into his death? [4]We were buried therefore with him by baptism into death, so that as Christ was raised from the dead by the glory of the Father, we too might walk in newness of life. (Romans 6:2-4)

Baptism, which Jesus had commanded (Matthew 28:19) so that people might be "saved" (Mark 16:16), has the power to forgive sins because through it, the Christian enters into the death and resurrection of Jesus Christ. Baptism contains a promise of eternal life: "For if we have been united with him in a death like his, we shall certainly be united with him in a resurrection like his" (Romans 6:5). It also allows for the forgiveness of sins and a new life of holiness:

> [6]We know that our old self was crucified with him so that the sinful body might be destroyed, and we might no longer be enslaved to sin. [7]For he who has died is freed from sin. [8]But if we have died with Christ, we believe that we shall also live with him. [9]For we know that Christ being raised from the dead will never die again; death no longer has dominion over him. [10]The death he died he died to sin, once for all, but the life he lives he lives to God. [11]So you

also must consider yourselves dead to sin and alive to God in Christ Jesus. [12]Let not sin therefore reign in your mortal bodies, to make you obey their passions. (Romans 6:6-12)

TAKEAWAY: *Because baptism is a participation in Christ's death and resurrection, the Christian receives the grace of dying to sin in order to live for God in Christ Jesus. Forgiveness of sins prepares for this new life of grace, virtue, and holiness.*

The Call to Forgive

Putting sin to death and being transformed in Christ mean that we are able to forgive people. Just as we were forgiven, so must we forgive. Sometimes that means putting to death our pride, anger, and resentment. And that brings us back to the parable of the unforgiving servant that we discussed in chapter 2 (Matthew 18:23-35).

One very important point that Jesus made in that parable is that our awareness of the greatness of the forgiveness we receive from God ought to motivate us to forgive people who offend us. This is all the more true when we consider that the price of our debt of sin is the suffering and death of Jesus Christ on the cross. As explained in chapter 2, the death of Jesus is the means of obtaining the forgiveness of our sins. This refers to the death of the completely innocent God-made-flesh, Jesus Christ. One way to deepen our awareness of what this means is to read each of the passion narratives in the Gospels: Matthew 26–27; Mark 14–15; Luke 22–23; and John 18–19. We can allow the images of Jesus Christ's suffering within these texts to fill our imagination so that we realize that reconciliation with God does not come cheaply. This can help us reflect that if the forgiveness of our sins was won because Christ suffered so much, then we can be all the more grateful for what we have received.

Another conclusion that Jesus wants us to draw from the parable, as well as from our reflection on Christ's suffering, is that we must become more generous in forgiving the people who have offended us. In his parable, Christ wants us to see that the forgiveness we receive from God is far greater than the forgiveness we offer other people. This understanding is based on the principle of the seriousness of sin depending on the status of the person who is offended. Our sins against God are so very serious because he is so great and infinite. When people offend me, they are offending a very limited person who also happens to be a sinner.

The experience of many of us is that we commonly become outraged and incensed that someone would offend and hurt us. We often emphasize that they had no right to offend us; we might claim that, at least in regard to them, we are innocent. Or if we are not completely innocent, at least they acted worse to us than we did to them. Like the unforgiving steward, we might be so opposed to letting go of the hurt that we refuse to forgive them.

Nonetheless, it is precisely at this point that Jesus summons us to forgive those who offend us, even if we are in the right. When telling the parable of the servant, Jesus did not deny that the other servant really owed him a hundred denarii. However, in light of the tremendous debt that had been forgiven him, he was obligated to forgive his fellow servant's debt. Because he refused to forgive the very small debt of his fellow servant, the lord in the parable called him a "wicked servant" (Matthew 18:32).

Jesus makes the same point earlier in Matthew's Gospel when he teaches his disciples how to pray. All Christians are familiar with this prayer:

> [9]"Our Father who art in heaven,
> Hallowed be thy name.
> [10]Thy kingdom come,
> Thy will be done,
> On earth as it is in heaven.
> [11]Give us this day our daily bread;
> [12]And forgive us our debts,
> As we also have forgiven our debtors;
> [13]And lead us not into temptation,
> But deliver us from evil." (Matthew 6:9-13)

Of course, verse 12 is the operative verse: "Forgive us our debts, / As we also have forgiven our debtors." The way we forgive other people is the norm by which the heavenly Father will forgive us. This is the basis for Jesus' later teaching in the parable of the unforgiving servant. In fact, Jesus emphasizes this teaching in the two verses that follow the prayer: "For if you forgive men their trespasses, your heavenly Father also will forgive you; but if you do not forgive men their trespasses, neither will your Father forgive your trespasses" (Matthew 6:14-15).

TAKEAWAY: *We must be generous in forgiving the people who have offended us. The way we forgive others is the norm by which our Father will forgive us.*

The last time I saw my grandmother, I asked her to show me her photo album so that I could learn the names of some of our relatives from Poland. Whenever she came to a picture of my grandfather, who died before I was born, she would immediately turn the page, slam it down, and call him a nasty word in Polish. I asked my grandmother, who was ninety-three at the time, "*Busia* (Polish for grandmother), do you want to die?"

"Yeah, sure, I'm tired," she answered.

"Then you have to forgive *Dziadziu*" (Polish for grandfather—I had never in my life addressed my grandparents by the English words). I knew many stories about how mean my grandfather had been to her before he abandoned her and her two small children in 1929.

She responded, "Don't talk crazy!"

I spoke to her in Polish, "Listen to what the Lord Jesus said: 'Forgive us our trespasses as we forgive those who trespass against us.'"

She reacted negatively, so I repeated the words again in Polish and paused. She slammed her hand on the table and said with some angry resignation, "Okay, I forgive him." This was hardly an enthusiastic embrace of Christ's principle of forgiveness as the premise of being forgiven by God, but it was a start. She died six months later, and I celebrated her funeral Mass more peacefully with the knowledge of this last conversation.

Jesus made this point in another passage about prayer:

[24]"Therefore I tell you, whatever you ask in prayer, believe that you received it, and you will. [25]And whenever you stand praying, forgive, if you have anything against any one; so

that your Father also who is in heaven may forgive you your trespasses." (Mark 11:24-25)

Here Jesus reaffirms the link between faith in God when we pray and forgiveness of one another as the basis of receiving forgiveness from our Father in heaven. This link is implied in the Lord's Prayer, since the petitions that surround the request for forgiveness all assume that the one praying has faith that God's kingdom will come, that his will can be done, and that he can provide our daily bread and keep us from evil. In the passage from Mark above, the link between faith and forgiveness is made more explicit.

St. Paul also teaches the need for forgiving one another: "Let all bitterness and wrath and anger and clamor and slander be put away from you, with all malice, and be kind to one another, tenderhearted, forgiving one another, as God in Christ forgave you" (Ephesians 4:31-32).

This exhortation, as well as the one in Colossians 3:12-13, explicitly summons the Christian to forgive just as God has forgiven us. Yet notice that St. Paul adds exhortations to include other virtues to this forgiveness—kindness and tenderheartedness, compassion, lowliness, meekness, and patience. These qualities are meant to temper the act of forgiveness, removing any "bitterness and wrath and anger and clamor," which are sometimes residual emotions present even as the act of forgiveness is chosen by the will. These virtues flow more easily into the act of forgiveness when we grow in humility. A proper humility stems from the realization that we are each sinners too and that our offenses against God are more serious than the offenses committed against us. This is not a humiliation that makes us think badly of ourselves but rather a humility that recognizes the deeper truths of the state of our souls before God our Lord. This kind of humility becomes a source of authentic peace as we accept the kind of truth about the human condition that Jesus Christ was teaching in the parable of the unforgiving servant.

–Questions for Reflection and Discussion–

1. Have you ever thought of battling sin by putting it "to death"? Why is that image useful for a Christian? How might it help you fight persistent patterns of sin in your life?

2. Do you see yourself as a new creation in Christ (2 Corinthians 5:17)? Why or why not?

3. Why is it important to have a personal relationship with the Lord in order to be transformed in his image? What is the role of the Holy Spirit in this process?

4. What does your baptism mean to you? How can you live it out on a practical level?

5. St. Paul lists other virtues that help us with forgiveness, including kindness, tenderheartedness, compassion, lowliness, meekness, and patience (Colossians 3:12-13). Why does he link these virtues with forgiveness? Which of these

qualities do you think are most important for you to grow in so that you can become a more forgiving person?

Chapter 9

Meditating on the Gospels

Goal of Chapter 9: *To pray about sin and allow God to address us and heal our souls.*

Scripture Highlights: *Mark 2:1-12; Matthew 9:9-13; Luke 7:36-50; 15:11-32; 19:1-10; John 4:4-42; 8:2-11*

If people today, living in a postmodern world, have difficulty talking about sin and incorporating it into their thinking, they certainly will have difficulty praying about sin. However, the Bible has much to offer in this regard, and so we will present some aspects of praying about sin. Of course, the double goal of this prayer will be to seek forgiveness for sins committed and to seek help in avoiding sin in the future. Such prayer becomes a graced way of learning to increase a person's consciousness of the fact that he or she has committed sin, which is a truth that in itself is quite healing.

One way of praying is to use St. Ignatius of Loyola's time-honored method of meditating on Bible narratives. We can do this with Gospel passages that deal with various aspects of sin, such as passages in which Jesus forgives sinners or teaches parables about forgiveness of sinners. The goal of such meditative prayer is to enter the Gospel scene and allow Christ to address our own souls with the same words. After using our imagination to vividly call to mind these various scenes, we are to move to a "colloquy," or dialogue, about the events.

St. Ignatius of Loyola recommends a triple colloquy in which we dialogue with the Blessed Virgin Mary, Jesus Christ, and God the Father. The assumption underlying all such prayer is that we ask the Holy Spirit of truth to guide each step of our meditation. In a certain sense, the Spirit remains invisible because he is turning the attention toward the Father, Jesus, and Mary. St. Ignatius recommends that we speak with these persons as a friend speaks to a friend. What would you say to each one about your meditation on the passage, and what might they say to you? Listen, and speak openly. End each colloquy with a prayer: the Hail Mary after the colloquy with the Blessed Virgin, the Anima Christi ("Soul of Christ," written by Ignatius) after the colloquy with Jesus Christ, and the Our Father after the colloquy with the Father.

For example, imagine Jesus on the cross as you stand there next to him. What would you say to him? What might he say to you? St. Ignatius recommends posing three questions as a way to begin this conversation: What have I done for Christ? What am I doing for Christ? What will I do for Christ? Answer each question honestly as you gaze upon Christ crucified, and imagine him talking back to you. Conclude the meditation with an Our Father.

Be sure to take enough time to pray these meditations. You might want to take one passage each day for your prayer time, or you might want to set aside a block of time to do a few at a time. Keep a journal and write down what you think the Lord may be saying to you during this time.

1. A Paralytic Goes through the Roof
(Mark 2:1-12)

After a short preaching tour in Galilee, Jesus returns to the home of Peter's mother-in-law in Capernaum, where he preaches the word to the people (Mark 2:1-2). Four men bring a paralytic on a pallet, and since they cannot bring him through the door, they open the roof and lower him into the room (2:3-4). "And when Jesus saw their faith, he said to the paralytic, 'My son, your sins are forgiven'" (2:5). Their faith results in action because they lower the paralytic through the roof, but that faith is focused on receiving a healing for their friend, not the forgiveness of sins. Jesus' words surprise them and shock the scribes: "Why does this man speak thus? It is blasphemy! Who can forgive sins but God alone?" (2:7). Jesus perceives their questioning, which expresses their doubt and shock. So he asks his own questions of them:

[8]"Why do you question thus in your hearts? [9]Which is easier, to say to the paralytic, 'Your sins are forgiven,' or to say, 'Rise, take up your pallet and walk'? [10]But that you may know that the Son of man has authority on earth to forgive sins"—he said to the paralytic—[11]"I say to you, rise, take up your pallet and go home." (Mark 2:8-11)

Judaism had no theological basis for allowing human beings to forgive sin; only God can forgive sins. The scribes explicitly teach this doctrine here. However, not only does Jesus claim to have the authority to forgive sins, but he proves it to them by healing the paralytic through a simple command: "Rise, take up your pallet and go home" (Mark 2:11). It is not yet possible for the scribes to understand that Jesus is God and therefore has the power to forgive as one aspect of his nature. However, they can see the miracle for themselves, a miracle that amazes everyone present and causes them to glorify God and say, "We never saw anything like this!" (2:12).

Imagine being this paralytic. Imagine yourself on the cot being lowered through the roof of the house, and sense the risk of trusting friends who love you enough to take such a bold step. When you hear Jesus say, "Your sins are forgiven," do you react with disappointment that it is not a physical healing, or do you feel a deep relief that sins you have not spoken about to others are perceived by Jesus and forgiven? Might you feel embarrassed that the forgiveness of your sin has been made in such a public forum? After Jesus heals you, what would you think about his power to forgive your sin?

2. Matthew the Tax Collector
(Matthew 9:9-13)

Tax collectors were a hated group in ancient Palestine. Observant Jews were not allowed to let them marry into their families. They not only worked for the Romans, gathering taxes for the oppressor, but they could keep for themselves anything they had collected over and above the amount demanded by the empire. This was doubly onerous for the poor. Nevertheless, Jesus will call two tax collectors to be his disciples. In this first example, Jesus takes the initiative:

> [9]As Jesus passed on from there, he saw a man called Matthew sitting at the tax office; and he said to him, "Follow me." And he rose and followed him. [10]And as he sat at table in the house, behold, many tax collectors and sinners came and sat down with Jesus and his disciples. [11]And when the Pharisees saw this, they said to his disciples, "Why does your teacher eat with tax collectors and sinners?" [12]But when he heard it, he said, "Those who are well have no need of a physician, but those who are sick. [13]Go and learn what this means, 'I desire mercy, and not sacrifice.' For I came not to call the righteous, but sinners." (Matthew 9:9-13; cf. Mark 2:13-17; Luke 5:27-32)

Note first that Jesus calls Matthew to follow him, and he leaves his tax collector's office behind, much as Peter, Andrew, James, and John had left their boats to follow Jesus. While those first four disciples left a simple but honest trade, Matthew left a more lucrative but dishonest profession behind. Second, the effect of the call was to bring Jesus and his disciples into Matthew's social world of tax collectors and sinners. Sharing table fellowship was much more than eating food; it was an acceptance of the society of the table, with its etiquette, interpersonal dynamics, and status within the larger society. For instance, the Mishnah and Talmud contain many rabbinic axioms about table fellowship among rabbis and their disciples, regulating seating arrangements—especially proximity to the rabbi—and roles of service while at table. This explains why the Pharisees were deeply scandalized by Jesus' fellowship with sinners.

In addition, an idea that was current among some of the Pharisees was that if each and every Jew would obey each and every precept of the law for only one hour, they would make a window of opportunity for the Messiah to come. This led them to conclude that each sinner bore responsibility not only for his or her sin but also for preventing the coming of the Messiah. Jesus responded to their being scandalized by stating that his mission was not to the righteous but to the sinners. In other words, the sinners did not prevent the coming of the Messiah but prompted it because they are precisely the people who need him. He supports his claim by citing Hosea 6:6: "I desire mercy and not sacrifice."

Finally, Matthew has already begun the work of evangelization by gathering together his associates in tax collecting and sin. Because of the rules of Jewish society, the other disciples would not have been very likely to meet, converse, or eat with that crowd, but it is easy for Matthew to bring Jesus into their circle. Oftentimes a converted sinner becomes very adept at winning over fellow sinners. He knows their idioms of speech, social conventions, faults, and fears from the inside, so he can address their concerns in ways that relate best to them. For example, many recovering alcoholics and drug users are marvelous at counseling other addicts.

Imagine yourself at Matthew's tax collection site. What is your level of surprise that Jesus has singled you out for discipleship, even though the rest of Jewish society legislates against fellowship with you? What kind of confidence do you have in Jesus to be able to invite other tax collectors and sinner friends to an event as important as table fellowship with Jesus? How do Jesus' words to the Pharisees, "I came not to call the righteous, but sinners" (Matthew 9:13), touch your own soul?

3. Zacchaeus (Luke 19:1-10)

The situation is a bit different with Zacchaeus of Jericho, the second tax collector that Jesus called. He was the "chief tax collector, and rich" (Luke 19:2). It was Zacchaeus who took the initiative to see Jesus, but he was too short to look over the heads of the crowd, among whom he was probably not too welcome. Therefore, "he ran on ahead and climbed up into a sycamore tree" along Jesus' way (19:3-4). As Jesus passed by, he turned to him and said, "Zacchaeus, make haste and come down; for I must stay at your house today." Then he "made haste and came down, and received him joyfully" (19:5-6). Once again, Jesus seeks table fellowship with a tax collector, and it causes great joy for the host, who would have been an outsider to religious society.

And again as well, Jesus' fellowship with a tax collector causes great scandal as the crowd murmurs that "he has gone in to be the guest of a man who is a sinner" (Luke 19:7). However, here Zacchaeus again takes the initiative in this situation, not with a theological principle, but with a demonstration of repentance: "Behold, Lord, the half of my goods I give to the poor; and if I have defrauded any one of anything, I restore it fourfold" (19:8). Zacchaeus gives half of his goods away to the poor; with the other half, he does a fourfold restitution for any fraud he has committed. The fourfold restitution follows the statute given in Exodus 22:1 for a stolen sheep. By the time he pays back all the restitution, the man who was once rich will have become impoverished. However, fellowship with Jesus is worth the loss of all his possessions in the world if he can gain eternal life. Therefore, Jesus responds to him, "Today salvation has come to this house, since he also is a son of Abraham" (19:9).

Picture yourself being short in stature, expecting no accommodation from the crowd because you are a despised tax collector. When you climb the sycamore tree, what do you expect to see? What do you expect to happen to you when Jesus walks by? Try to experience the surprise when Jesus asks to dine with you rather than any of the other upright citizens of Jericho. When people publicly criticize your life as a sinful tax collector, what is your first feeling? What causes you to publicly state your generosity to the poor and decide to make restitution for your past corruption? How do you react to Jesus' words, "Today salvation has come to this house, since he also is a son of Abraham. For the Son of man came to seek and to save the lost" (Luke 19:9-10)? What does Jesus' promise of salvation mean to you?

4. A Woman Washes Jesus' Feet
(Luke 7:36-50)

Jesus shared table fellowship with the Pharisees more often than with the tax collectors, and it often became the scene of disputes with these scholars of the law. On one occasion, a Pharisee named Simon invited him to table, which became the scene of the great conversion of a sinner:

> [37]And behold, a woman of the city, who was a sinner, when she learned that he was sitting at table in the Pharisee's house, brought an alabaster flask of ointment, [38]and standing behind him at his feet, weeping, she began to wet his feet with her tears, and wiped them with the hair of her head, and kissed his feet, and anointed them with the ointment. (Luke 7:37-38)

This woman's actions are extravagant. Women did not normally share table fellowship, even when they had good reputations. This woman was a known sinner who would not have had any kind of fellowship with a leading Pharisee, so her presence was a surprise, to say the least. She sheds tears of repentance so copiously that they wet Jesus' feet. Women who care about their appearance usually spend time caring for their hair; this one wipes Jesus' dusty feet with her hair. Finally, she shares one of her most precious objects with Jesus—an alabaster jar of ointment. Alabaster is a translucent stone from which a very expensive jar can be formed by drilling into it, as is still done in Egypt. Such a jar could hold a very expensive and precious ointment that would last a woman a long time, much like very expensive perfume does today. However, she lavishly pours it out on Jesus as a further sign of her repentance.

Simon the Pharisee is scandalized by this scene and says to himself, "If this man were a prophet, he would have known who and what sort of woman this is who is touching him, for she is a sinner" (Luke 7:39). Although Simon says nothing out loud, Jesus answers his thought with his own question:

> [41] "A certain creditor had two debtors; one owed five hundred denarii, and the other fifty. [42] When they could not pay, he forgave them both. Now which of them will love him more?" [43] Simon answered, "The one, I suppose, to whom he forgave more." And he said to him, "You have judged rightly." (Luke 7:41-43)

The little parable assumes that sin is similar to a debt, as Jesus had taught in his prayer, "Forgive us our debts, as we also have forgiven our debtors" (Matthew 6:12) and in the parable of the unforgiving servant (18:23-35). Jesus then turns toward the woman and applies the parable to Simon and to her:

> [44] "Do you see this woman? I entered your house, you gave me no water for my feet, but she has wet my feet with her tears and wiped them with her hair. [45] You gave me no kiss, but from the time I came in she has not ceased to kiss my feet. [46] You did not anoint my head with oil, but she has anointed my feet with ointment. [47] Therefore I tell you, her

sins, which are many, are forgiven, for she loved much; but he who is forgiven little, loves little." (Luke 7:44-47)

His last line contains two distinct points. First, her many sins are forgiven because "she loved much." Her lavish kindness to Jesus not only contrasts with the poor hospitality shown him by his host but also flows from her own desire to show him her love. This love by a human calls forth God's mercy in return and brings her forgiveness of her sins. Second, a person who has few sins forgiven loves God little in return. The sense of having little forgiven may derive not so much from the actual sins forgiven but from the sinner's lack of appreciation of the seriousness of the sin or of the greatness of the freely-given reconciliation with God (as in the case of the unforgiving servant).

Jesus then becomes the cause of scandal at the table when he tells the woman, "Your sins are forgiven" (Luke 7:48). Just as the Pharisees were shocked at Jesus' offer of forgiveness of sins to the paralytic (Mark 2:7), so were the people at Simon's table: "Who is this, who even forgives sins?" (Luke 7:49). Jesus ignores their question about his identity and its relation to his power to forgive sins. (Readers of Luke's whole Gospel are expected to answer the question in light of the angel Gabriel's revelation at the Annunciation that Jesus is the Son of God.) Instead, Jesus addresses the woman and says, "Your faith has saved you; go in peace" (7:50).

While his answer to Simon earlier (in Luke 7:47) attributed the woman's forgiveness to her love, here Jesus attributes her salvation to her faith. This link between love and faith brings to mind

St. Paul's reference to "faith working through love" (Galatians 5:6). Never do these two virtues work against each other; instead, they work together and are closely allied with hope, the third theological virtue: "For through the Spirit, by faith, we wait for the hope of righteousness" (5:5).

Imagine the scene at Simon's home when Jesus comes to dinner. Do you see yourself as one of the guests at table or as the woman who washes Jesus' feet with her tears? Have you ever been filled with so much regret for sin that you actually shed tears? What attitudes accompanied your repentance that caused you to weep over your sin? What might make a person pour out one of her most valuable possessions—ointment in an alabaster jar—on Jesus' feet? Can you place yourself in her state of both humility and generosity? What would it feel like to have Jesus tell a parable that defends your action? When he declares your sins forgiven, what is your reaction? After he says your faith has saved you, what do you discover about the quality and meaning of your faith? Is it strong? Does it need nurturing? Does it need guidance to know better what to believe?

5. The Samaritan Woman at the Well (John 4:4-42)

On his return to Galilee from Jerusalem, Jesus and the disciples pass through Samaria and rest at Jacob's well near the city of Sychar (John 4:4-6). He begins a dialogue with a Samaritan woman by asking her for a drink of water. She is taken aback because Jews and Samaritans have no dealings with each other due to ongoing enmity between them (4:7-9).

Jesus takes the conversation a level deeper by saying, "If you knew the gift of God, and who it is that is saying to you, 'Give me a drink,' you would have asked him and he would have given you living water" (John 4:10). His offer of living water goes over her head, and she responds on a very practical level, "Sir, you have nothing to draw with, and the well is deep; where do you get that living water? Are you greater than our father Jacob, who gave us the well, and drank from it himself, and his sons, and his cattle?" (4:11-12). Her second question shows that she can recognize greatness only on the level of providing water the way Jacob had done. Jesus takes her deeper still by pointing out the limitations of the water from Jacob's well in contrast to the water he can offer: "Every one who drinks of this water will thirst again, but whoever drinks of the water that I shall give him will never thirst; the water that I shall give him will become in him a spring of water welling up to eternal life" (4:13-14).

The scene takes a new turn when she at last accepts his offer: "Sir, give me this water, that I may not thirst, nor come here to draw" (John 4:15). Jesus then addresses her life situation: "Go, call your husband, and come here." She says, "I have no husband." Jesus responds, "You are right in saying, 'I have no husband'; for you have had five husbands, and he whom you now have is not your husband; this you said truly" (4:16-18). Notice that he does not accuse her of lying to him; rather, he agrees with the statement on its own level, but then lays out the actual facts of her misbehavior. Presented with this truth about her life, she responds, "Sir, I perceive that you are a prophet" (4:19).

The next stage in the discussion is her theological dodge in which she changes the subject to ask about the differences between Samaritan and Jewish worship. Jesus speaks the truth that "salvation is from the Jews" (John 4:22), but that ultimately, "the hour is coming, and now is, when the true worshipers will worship the Father in spirit and truth, for such the Father seeks to worship him. God is spirit, and those who worship him must worship in spirit and truth" (4:23-24). She responds again with another theological assertion: "I know that Messiah is coming (he who is called Christ); when he comes, he will show us all things" (4:25). Jesus responds with an unexpected revelation: "I who speak to you am he" (4:26). This encounter with Jesus, who knows her sins, transforms her into an evangelist: "So the woman left her water jar, and went away into the city, and said to the people, 'Come, see a man who told me all that I ever did. Can this be the Christ?'" (4:28-29).

Put yourself in the place of a Samaritan trained to believe that Jews reject you. You happen upon a Jewish man resting near the well where you have come to draw water. What would be your first thoughts when he initiates a conversation? Consider each stage of his conversation, as he takes you to deeper meanings through a number of odd requests and statements. What is your reaction when he tells you to call your spouse, but you know the embarrassing truth that you are living with a person to whom you are not married? Have you ever experienced a conversation, lecture, or sermon that pointed to a sinful area of life, causing you great embarrassment or shame? Did you dodge the issue or bring it directly to Jesus? Pay attention to the way Jesus accepts her, answers her questions more deeply than she has asked them, and reveals his identity as the Messiah to her. How does this revelation of himself affect you?

6. The Woman Caught in Adultery
(John 8:2-11)

Jesus is again in Jerusalem, teaching in the Temple, when the scribes and Pharisees bring to him a woman who has been caught in the act of adultery. The Pharisees ask him, "Now in the law Moses commanded us to stone such. What do you say about her?" (John 8:5).They are using her situation to test Jesus and bring a charge against him (8:6a). In silence Jesus begins to write on the ground with his finger as they press the issue. Only then does he say, "Let him who is without sin among you be the first to throw a stone at her" (8:7). He returns to his writing on the ground as the accusers leave "one by one, beginning with the eldest," until "Jesus was left alone with the woman standing before him" (8:8-9). Jesus then asks her, "Woman, where are they? Has no one condemned you?" She says, "No one, Lord." And Jesus replies, "Neither do I condemn you; go, and do not sin again" (8:10-11).

No one knows what Jesus wrote on the ground, but St. Jerome speculated that he wrote the sins of the accusers, beginning with the eldest. The realization that the accusers are themselves sinners makes them unqualified to condemn the woman. This is consistent with Jesus' teaching in Matthew and Luke: "Judge not, that you be not judged. For with the judgment you pronounce you will be judged" (Matthew 7:1-2; cf. Luke 6:37-38). Jesus does not condemn the woman for her past sin, but he says the same thing to her that he said to the paralytic, "Go, and do not sin again." He neither condemns nor condones; he summons her to virtue as the goal of having received forgiveness.

Picture Jesus teaching people in the Temple when the scribes and the Pharisees bring the woman caught in adultery to him. Imagine being the woman whose once private and intimate sin is brought to public attention and now faces a threat of imminent death. What would go through your mind as Jesus gives permission for the one without sin to cast the first stone? What would the wait feel like? What would you think as each man leaves the scene until you are alone with Jesus? Hear Jesus tell you, "Neither do I condemn you; go, and do not sin again" (John 8:11). What would you decide to do in order to avoid sinning again? Have a conversation with Jesus about the steps you must take to stop sinning.

7. The Loving Father
(or the Prodigal Son) (Luke 15:11-32)

The third parable in Luke 15 is quite long and complicated in depicting the joy of heaven over the sinner's repentance versus the resentment of the self-righteous.

[11]And he said, "There was a man who had two sons; [12]and the younger of them said to his father, 'Father, give me the share of property that falls to me.' And he divided his living between them." (Luke 15:11-12).

The opening of the parable mentions the man with two sons. This father is the main character throughout both parts of the parable as he deals with each of his sons. According to the Book of Sirach, it was possible to distribute the inheritance upon death (which 33:23 recommends) or while still alive (which 33:19-21 discourages). According to Deuteronomy, one should "acknowledge the first-born . . . by giving him a double portion of all that he has, for he is the first issue of his strength; the right of the first-born is his" (21:17). Since the older son would normally receive twice as much as the other sons, this younger son receives one-third of his father's property.

[13]"Not many days later, the younger son gathered all he had and took his journey into a far country, and there he squandered his property in loose living. [14]And when he had spent everything, a great famine arose in that country, and

he began to be in want. ¹⁵So he went and joined himself to one of the citizens of that country, who sent him into his fields to feed swine. ¹⁶And he would gladly have fed on the pods that the swine ate; and no one gave him anything." (Luke 15:13-16)

For a while this son lived "high off the hog," spending everything on his own pleasure rather than living responsibly. His prodigality and a famine beyond his control bring him lower than the hogs. Being reduced to a swineherd introduces a degree of shame; such labor was degrading and did not even provide enough for his basic need for food. In this state he speaks a soliloquy that contrasts the state of his father's servants with his own miserable condition.

¹⁷"But when he came to himself he said, 'How many of my father's hired servants have bread enough and to spare, but I perish here with hunger! ¹⁸I will arise and go to my father, and I will say to him, "Father, I have sinned against heaven and before you; ¹⁹I am no longer worthy to be called your son; treat me as one of your hired servants."'" (Luke 15:17-19)

His realization of his misery becomes the turning point in his conversion. Alcoholics and drug addicts call this "hitting bottom." "Bottom" varies for everyone because the balance of tolerable pain and the willingness to change one's life is a changing spectrum from one person to another, or even within the life span of the same individual.

At this point, the father comes into prominence and remains central throughout the rest of the parable.

> [20]"And he arose and came to his father. But while he was yet at a distance, his father saw him and had compassion, and ran and embraced him and kissed him. [21]And the son said to him, 'Father, I have sinned against heaven and before you; I am no longer worthy to be called your son.' [22]But the father said to his servants, 'Bring quickly the best robe, and put it on him; and put a ring on his hand, and shoes on his feet; [23]and bring the fatted calf and kill it, and let us eat and make merry; [24]for this my son was dead, and is alive again; he was lost, and is found.' And they began to make merry." (Luke 15:20-24)

At this initial stage of conversion, the son can recognize only the justice of his situation. He has foolishly wasted one-third of his father's hard-earned property, impoverished himself, and degraded his status in society. On the other hand, the father exudes compassion and mercy, manifested by his running out to meet the son, embracing and kissing him, giving him the best robe, a ring, and sandals, and ordering a feast. Blessed John Paul II recognized these signs of the father's affection for the son, who was once dead and lost but is now alive and found, as a manifestation of a mercy that exceeds justice. Were the father to accept the younger son's terms of justice, then he would merely have another hired servant. By showing mercy in throwing a feast with merrymaking, the father retains his identity as a father because he has restored his son to a proper filial state. So also does God's mercy to sinners restore them to the image and likeness of God that they were intended to be from their first moment of existence. They are even taught by Jesus to call God their Father (Matthew 6:9; Luke 11:2; cf. Romans 8:15 and Galatians 4:6).

The final section of the parable relates back to the initial problem in Luke 15:1-2, in which the Pharisees and scribes object to Jesus eating with tax collectors and sinners:

> [25]"Now his elder son was in the field; and as he came and drew near to the house, he heard music and dancing. [26]And he called one of the servants and asked what this meant. [27]And he said to him, 'Your brother has come, and your father has killed the fatted calf, because he has received him safe and sound.' [28]But he was angry and refused to go in. His father came out and entreated him, [29]but he answered his father, 'Lo, these many years I have served you, and I never disobeyed your command; yet you never gave me a kid, that I might make merry with my friends. [30]But when this son of yours came, who has devoured your living with harlots, you killed for him the fatted calf!' [31]And he said to him, 'Son, you are always with me, and all that is mine is yours. [32]It was fitting to make merry and be glad, for this your brother was dead, and is alive; he was lost, and is found.'" (Luke 15:25-32)

The father's good news about his lost son who is now found is experienced as bad news by the older son. His anger at the injustice of celebrating a prodigal son keeps him from entering into the fellowship with the rest of the household. The father comes out to him, much as he had run out to meet the returning prodigal, but he is met with the older son's logic based on justice. He asserts that he has always obeyed all of his father's orders, so he deserves better treatment. He also points out that he has never been rewarded with even a goat for a celebration with his friends; this would be far less costly than the fatted calf butchered for the returning prodigal. Because he is not able to accept his younger brother, he calls him "this son of yours." He stays focused on the sins of the younger son whom, he says, has devoured the father's (and his) property.

The father concludes the parable with two points. First, the older son is always his son, and that relationship is not jeopardized simply because the younger son is now reconciled to the father. The property is all his, so his rights under the law are not endangered. Second, the return of the younger son is an event of great magnitude—he had been dead and lost and now he is alive and found. The merrymaking is a fitting response to this transformation of a sinner.

Put yourself in the place of the prodigal son and examine yourself for the attitudes that would motivate you to take your portion of your inheritance before your father's death and go to a different country. What would you hope to achieve by such a move? Have you ever taken steps to do something parallel to this? What would you be thinking as you spent your wealth in such a way? Have you ever found yourself in a state in which you wasted your personal resources on "loose living"? Did you feel the kind of despondency that the son experienced? Compare your thoughts in that state to the son's thoughts. If your father were waiting for you to welcome you, what would you think? Imagine the new clothes, sandals and ring, the reintroduction to familiar members of the household, and the waiting for the feast. Would you have expected this kind of welcome as a sinner? What would you think of your brother's reaction? Was it more along the lines of what you had originally expected upon your return?

Another approach is to consider this parable from the perspective of the older brother. What would you think about the younger brother taking his portion of the wealth and leaving the household? Examine your attitudes about his return and the father's celebration. If you heard your father's plea to accept your returned brother, what would you decide to do? The older son's response is not included in the parable. This lack of a conclusion is meant to evoke a response from the listener: will you hold on to simple justice and end the relationship with the younger brother because he has sinned? Or will you learn to rejoice in mercy, as the father has done, and receive the sinner back into a relationship as brother?

You may also repeat your meditation of this parable by putting yourself in the place of the father. What would you think if your son left you so foolishly, as the prodigal did? What would be your expectations that would motivate you to keep on the lookout for his return? What interior attitude would allow you to accept him back into the household so fully? What would you hope to achieve in the conversation with the older brother who has never left?

8. The Pharisee and the Publican (Luke 18:9-14)

This next parable is addressed to those self-righteous people who despise sinners and uses two different men as examples of how to be justified:

> [9]He also told this parable to some who trusted in themselves that they were righteous and despised others: [10]"Two men went up into the temple to pray, one a Pharisee and the other a tax collector. [11]The Pharisee stood and prayed thus with himself, 'God, I thank thee that I am not like other men, extortioners, unjust, adulterers, or even like this tax collector. [12]I fast twice a week, I give tithes of all that I get.' [13]But the tax collector, standing far off, would not even lift up his eyes to heaven, but beat his breast, saying, 'God, be merciful to me a sinner!' [14]I tell you, this man went down to his house justified rather than the other; for every one who exalts himself will be humbled, but he who humbles himself will be exalted." (Luke 18:9-14)

The Pharisee prays with a good deal of self-confidence, standing in the Temple and offering thanks to God. The first thing for which he gives thanks is that he is "not like other men." His first list gives thanks that he is not an extortioner, unjust person, or adulterer—a list that is based on the Ten Commandments. He points out that he is not like the nearby tax collector. As noted in the stories about Matthew and Zacchaeus, tax collectors were particularly despised and avoided. Next, he lists two positive things he does: he fasts twice a week and tithes everything. While the Old Testament law required fasting on the Day of Atonement and Jewish custom required a few other days each year, fasting twice a week was far beyond the normal expectation of an observant Jew. One cannot but notice that his "thanksgiving" has quickly turned attention from the God he thanks to the things he himself has accomplished. He even uses his prayer to commit the deadly sin of pride—looking down on other people. He cannot enjoy the gifts God has given him without comparing himself favorably to other people. A stance of looking down on others requires one to turn away from looking up to God, which is itself the proper stance of humility.

The tax collector does not physically turn his eyes to heaven; he feels too embarrassed to do so because he is aware of his sins. However, his heart is turned to God as he simply addresses him, saying as he beats his breast, "God, be merciful to me a sinner!" He recognizes that he depends on mercy. He cannot convince God of anything by contrasting himself with other sinners. The norm for righteousness is not set by human beings but by God. Like the tax collector, we are all sinners in comparison to Jesus, and we are all in need of God's mercy. The fact is, the more honestly and humbly we admit our guilt and ask for his mercy, the more readily God gives it to us.

This parable highlights one of the real surprises in my own spiritual growth. The sisters who taught me, and later the teachers at the minor seminary where I went to high school, set before us students a number of high ideals for the moral and spiritual life. They themselves were good examples, and I wanted to imitate them because their actions rang true to their words. I got the idea in my mind that I needed to achieve these moral and spiritual ideals if I was to have a good relationship with God. However, I also knew myself to be somewhat lazy about them, especially if they did not seem convenient to my immediate plans for a particular day.

After entering the Jesuit order and making the Spiritual Exercises of St. Ignatius of Loyola, I gradually learned that I could not pretend to be as virtuous as I had hoped in my ideals. I needed to search my conscience more thoroughly, stop blaming other people or my life's circumstances for my continuing faults, and admit fully that I am the only one responsible for the sins I commit. They do not happen to me; I do them. This admission of guilt and responsibility was rather scary to me, but I had to accept that it was true. The amazing thing is that the more honestly I admitted my sins and took responsibility for them, the more peace I found in my prayer. As I confessed them privately to God and then brought them to the Sacrament of Reconciliation, I found far more interior peace than I had when I tried to think that I was better than I was. This parable about the Pharisee and the tax collector came alive for me. The forgiving grace of Christ reached sins that I had tried to keep away from God; when I could admit them, I could seek his mercy.

Put yourself in the place of the Pharisee. Why do you look at the tax collector when you are praying and not at God? How does it make you feel when you look down on others? Do you get momentary pleasure? Why is your fasting and tithing so uppermost in your mind? Do you feel God should take notice of you because of that? Do you believe that God loves you for who you are, not for what you do? Do you believe he loves the tax collector as much as he loves you? Repent of your sins of pride, and ask God to help you pray the prayer of the tax collector.

Now put yourself in the place of the tax collector. Do you feel you need mercy from God? Do you pray his prayer? Take the time to experience God's mercy.

Meditating on the Psalms

Goal of Chapter 10: *To pray the penitential psalms in order to experience the emotions and attitudes of the psalmist.*

Scripture Highlights: *Psalms 6; 32; 38; 51; 103; 130*

Another way to pray about sin is by using the psalms. The Book of Psalms is a collection of prayers from ancient Israel that were used primarily in the Temple liturgy. There are many diferent types of of psalms—psalms of praise, thanksgiving, wisdom, laments, and historical over-views—that were composed to deal with the many different needs in prayer. The Church has designated certain psalms as "penitential," that is, appropriate for prayer during a time of personal or communal repentance. These psalms take the form of laments because their subject is lamenting over sin and the problems that arise for the sinner.

One suggestion is that we pray these psalms as a preparation for Confession or as a penance, entering into the various attitudes and strong feelings expressed by the psalmists.

1. Psalm 6

Two psalms—Psalm 6 and Psalm 38, which follows—treat the theme of the sick sinner. Psalm 6 was used in the Jewish daily liturgy as a prayer of penitence and is used in the Church's liturgy today. The lament of the individual in time of sickness is appropriate to the First Week of the Spiritual Exercises, since St. Ignatius suggests that we see ourselves as sick persons roaming the world.

> ¹O LORD, rebuke me not in thy anger,
>   nor chasten me in thy wrath.
> ²Be gracious to me, O LORD, for I am languishing;
>   O LORD, heal me, for my bones are troubled.

Verses 1-2 consist of both negative and positive petitions. First, the psalmist asks the Lord not to rebuke or chasten him, since a person cannot hold up under the power of God's wrath. Then he asks for grace and healing because he is "languishing," which translates a Hebrew word meaning to "droop" or "hang down" one's head. The word "troubled" is a strong term ranging from "disturbed" to "terrified" and appears in the next verse:

> ³My soul also is sorely troubled.
>   But thou, O LORD—how long?

The description of both bones and soul being terrified indicates that this feeling comes from deep inside the person. When we pray these verses, we can reflect on those fears that come from deep inside us and then turn to God and ask, "How long?"

⁴Turn, O LORD, save my life;
    deliver me for the sake of thy steadfast love.

The psalmist does not dwell overly long on the question "How long?" because he is more interested in petitioning the Lord to save his life and deliver him "for the sake of thy steadfast love." *Hesed* is the word translated as "steadfast love." The word describes the covenant relationship and refers to the kind of love that exists when someone has made a covenant commitment, as distinct from *ahabah*, the more common word for "love."

⁵For in death there is no remembrance of thee;
    in Sheol who can give thee praise?

In verse 5 the psalmist appeals to God's interests: if the psalmist dies, he will go to Sheol, the place of the dead, where no one can praise God. A Christian has the hope of eternal life in heaven where the soul praises God for all eternity. However, the sinner who prays this psalm may also have a legitimate fear of hell, where no praise will be possible. With that prospect in mind, the Christian can correctly pray to remain in this life to repent of past and current sin, make reparation for it, and seek to live out the holiness that shapes us into the image and likeness of God.

⁶I am weary with my moaning;
    every night I flood my bed with tears;
    I drench my couch with my weeping.
⁷My eye wastes away because of grief,
    it grows weak because of all my foes.

Verses 6-7 return to a description of the psalmist's pain, which is less an attempt to tell God what he already knows than a way to sink into the sorrow so that the psalmist recognizes his own pain. Some speak of the necessity of "hitting bottom"—when life becomes so miserable and the pain is so great that a person is willing to seek a change.

> [8]Depart from me, all you workers of evil;
> for the LORD has heard the sound of my weeping.
> [9]The LORD has heard my supplication;
> the LORD accepts my prayer.
> [10]All my enemies shall be ashamed and sorely troubled;
> they shall turn back, and be put to shame in
> a moment.

The psalmist concludes with a prayer of confidence that the Lord has already heard his prayer. Such confidence characterizes faith: even when our "enemies" may still be present—which for the Christian could be sin, Satan, or illness—the person of faith begins to believe that the Lord will give him the victory. These enemies will be "sorely troubled," the same words that described the feeling in his own bones and soul in verses 2-3.

2. Psalm 38

This lament of the individual in time of sickness, similar to Psalm 6, has become a favorite of recovering alcoholics and drug addicts, especially as they experience withdrawal symptoms. The superscription calls this "A Psalm of David, for the memorial offering." There were two kinds of memorial sacrifices: the cereal and oil offering mixed with incense (cf. Leviticus 2:1-10) and the burning of the incense placed on the showbread every Sabbath (24:7). In Scripture, the use of the word "remembrance" (except for one case in Wisdom 16:6) refers to sacrifice. When Jesus at the Last Supper said, "Do this in remembrance of me" (Luke 22:19), he was not merely asking the apostles to recall him to mind; he was also referring to his sacrifice on the cross.

Christians can bring the fruit of praying this psalm to the Holy Sacrifice of the Mass in powerful ways. At the offertory, as the bread and wine are presented to the priest, we can offer the sufferings considered during the psalm along with the bread and wine. Just as the wheat and grapes were crushed, then baked or fermented to form bread and wine, so also does the pain of life crush, bake, and ferment us. When the priest speaks the words of consecration, "This is my Body" and "This is the chalice of my Blood," the bread and wine that are offered become the Body and Blood of Jesus Christ. That moment of Mass re-presents Christ's sacrifice on Calvary in an unbloody way, and all of the sufferings we spiritually attached to the bread and wine become united with Jesus' suffering and death.

At Holy Communion, which is the sign of the resurrection of Jesus, we receive him into our hearts with a hope that just as his death led to his resurrection, so will our sufferings lead to the salvation that God has in store for us. We, too, will live out his death and resurrection in an intimate communion with the Lord all along the way.

> [1]O LORD, rebuke me not in thy anger,
>   nor chasten me in thy wrath!

Here, as in Psalm 6:1, the petition betrays a common assumption that God is punishing the sinner for past sins through the experiences of pain and sickness. We may feel that God has singled us out for particular punishment. In fact, God warns us against various sins because they have dangerous or even deadly consequences. We do better if we see that God warns us against committing sin because he knows we were not made for such abuse to our person. He is trying to protect us from the effects of sin, much like a parent tries to protect a small child from playing with matches or running into the street.

Verses 2-8 are a description of the pain and misery the sinner is feeling. Substance abusers often find this psalm very poignant because in their own suffering, they can relate to the psalmist's pain:

> [2]For thy arrows have sunk into me,
>   and thy hand has come down on me.
> [3]There is no soundness in my flesh
>   because of thy indignation;
> there is no health in my bones
>   because of my sin.

⁴For my iniquities have gone over my head;
    they weigh like a burden too heavy for me.
⁵My wounds grow foul and fester
    because of my foolishness,
⁶I am utterly bowed down and prostrate;
    all the day I go about mourning.
⁷For my loins are filled with burning,
    and there is no soundness in my flesh.
⁸I am utterly spent and crushed;
    I groan because of the tumult of my heart.

After this description of pain, he turns to the Lord in direct prayer, recognizing that God knows his suffering:

⁹Lord, all my longing is known to thee,
    my sighing is not hidden from thee.
¹⁰My heart throbs, my strength fails me;
    and the light of my eyes—it also has gone from me.

The psalmist's statement of faith that the Lord knows his suffering is more powerful for those who recall the passion, suffering, and death of Jesus Christ. They can relate their suffering to his and join their own pain with his.

Next, the psalmist describes the radical loneliness he feels as friends abandon him and enemies seek to harm him:

¹¹My friends and companions stand aloof from my plague,
    and my kinsmen stand afar off.

^{12}Those who seek my life lay their snares,
    those who seek my hurt speak of ruin,
    and meditate treachery all the day long.

This isolation is made worse by his inability to receive communication or return it:

^{13}But I am like a deaf man, I do not hear,
    like a dumb man who does not open his mouth.
^{14}Yea, I am like a man who does not hear,
    and in whose mouth are no rebukes.

In verses 15-17 he makes an act of faith that the Lord will answer him in the midst of his pain:

^{15}But for thee, O Lord, do I wait;
    it is thou, O Lord my God, who wilt answer.
^{16}For I pray, "Only let them not rejoice over me,
    who boast against me when my foot slips!"
^{17}For I am ready to fall,
    and my pain is ever with me.

The first step of the Twelve Step program is to recognize that "I am powerless over alcohol"—or drugs, sex, pornography, gambling, shopping, overeating, or any other addictive behavior. Only when we interiorly accept that powerlessness over sin can we make an act of faith that God is more powerful than our sin (the second step) and then turn to the Lord directly and ask for help (the third step).

Verse 18 is a key turning point. The psalmist changes his focus from his pain to his own guilt and responsibility for having sinned:

[18]I confess my iniquity,
    I am sorry for my sin.

The fourth of the Twelve Steps is to make a thorough moral inventory of my life. This entails an acceptance that God's moral laws are true, good, and binding on me. I have no exemption clause to excuse me from obeying God's law. Then I take personal responsibility for the infractions of that law that I have committed. This is my "iniquity," a word derived from a root meaning to be "bent." While God seeks for us to be morally "upright" or straight, our moral failures bend and misshape us. In Hebrew, the word "sin" means to "miss the mark" (the same meaning for sin in Greek), a term derived from missing a target with arrows. By committing sin, I miss the goals of life that God has set for me, and I must take personal responsibility for that and repent.

The psalmist returns to his troubles, especially those caused by his enemies:

[19]Those who are my foes without cause are mighty,
    and many are those who hate me wrongfully.
[20]Those who render me evil for good
    are my adversaries because I follow after good.

He concludes with a final petition for help in a negative and a positive form:

²¹Do not forsake me, O LORD!
  O my God, be not far from me!
²²Make haste to help me, O Lord, my salvation!

The psalmist requests that he not be forsaken and distant from God, which is what he feels in all the pain he has described in the preceding verses. On the positive side, he asks God to "make haste" and help him, a petition that includes a statement of faith that God is his salvation.

This psalm can help any suffering sinner face the realities of the pain caused by sin. It leads us to recognize our responsibility for our sins, and it helps us to place our faith in God. It is the Lord who saves those who repent by forgiving our sins, giving us the grace to lead a life of holiness, and offering us companionship and intimacy, which lead to eternal life.

3. Psalm 51

This psalm is one of the most poignant descriptions of sin and repentance in the Psalter. The superscription identifies a specific event as the background of its composition: "A Psalm of David, when Nathan the prophet came to him after he had gone in to Bathsheba." The Second Book of Samuel tells the story of David's sin of adultery with Bathsheba, the wife of Uriah, who was fighting David's war with the Ammonites. After a failed attempt to arrange for Uriah to be with his wife so that he would think her child was his own, David sent orders for Uriah to be sent to the front lines of the army and thus die in battle so that David could claim Bathsheba as his wife (2 Samuel 11:2-27). After this double breach of the Ten Commandments, the prophet Nathan confronted David, who repented of his sin (12:1-15).

A close examination and meditation on these texts from 2 Samuel are well worth the time. Just as David had been highly favored and blessed by God, so can many of us reflect on the blessings God has given us. We can also reflect that just as David, though surrounded by many blessings, broke the commandments, so also do many of us break God's moral law without consideration of all he has done for us. David repented, and Psalm 51 is an apt prayer of repentance, used by Israel and the Church for millennia to express sorrow for sin.

The prayer begins with parallel petitions for mercy:

[1]Have mercy on me, O God,
    according to thy steadfast love;

> according to thy abundant mercy blot out my
> transgressions.
> [2]Wash me thoroughly from my iniquity,
>   and cleanse me from my sin!

Petitions begin and end the first verse, with two norms of forgiveness being set out in between—a literary structure known as *chiasmus*, a favorite device in Israelite literature. The norm for forgiveness is not raw justice; that would destroy the sinner. As in the parable of the unforgiving servant (Matthew 18:23-35), no human being is able to repay God for the debt of sin according to norms of strict justice. Rather, the Lord's "steadfast love" (*hesed*), or covenant love, and his mercy are the norm. At this point, the Christian can aptly recall St. Paul's Letter to the Ephesians: "But God, who is rich in mercy, out of the great love with which he loved us, even when we were dead through our trespasses, made us alive together with Christ" (2:4-5).

Next comes a confession of guilt:

> [3]For I know my transgressions,
>   and my sin is ever before me.

The psalmist begins with an admission of personal guilt for his sins. The word "transgressions" translates a Hebrew word meaning "rebellions," a term used for political uprisings against the king. When referring to moral failure, it is the most serious term for sin, conveying the type of conscious rejection of the Lord's authority that is akin to the concept of mortal sin. The other term used for "sin," as noted in Psalm 38, means to "miss the mark." The repetition of terms is an acceptance of the seriousness of the sin.

> [4]Against thee, thee only, have I sinned,
>> and done that which is evil in thy sight,
> so that thou art justified in thy sentence
>> and blameless in thy judgment.

Verse 4 understands the misdeed from the perspective of faith: it is not merely a *faux pas* but a sin directly against God. Though David's offenses of adultery and murder did irreparable harm to Uriah, it was God's commandments that he broke, so God is fully justified in pronouncing sentence against him.

> [5]Behold, I was brought forth in iniquity,
>> and in sin did my mother conceive me.

This recognition that sin goes back to the origin of life sets the context of sin in the state of human fallenness. Each person who prays this text can reflect on this fact while at the same time joining the psalmist in recognizing personal responsibility for the individual sinful acts he or she commits.

Then follows a series of petitions that describe the desired state of reconciliation with God:

> [6]Behold, thou desirest truth in the inward being;
>> therefore teach me wisdom in my secret heart.

We humans are created with a craving for the truth; this is yet another aspect of being created in the image and likeness of God, who is truth personified (cf. John 14:6; 8:31-32). Since God desires the truth at the core of our being, the psalmist prays that God teach wisdom within his heart. Wisdom is a gift from God and will lead to knowing the truth.

> [7]Purge me with hyssop, and I shall be clean;
>> wash me, and I shall be whiter than snow.
> [8]Fill me with joy and gladness;
>> let the bones which thou hast broken rejoice.
> [9]Hide thy face from my sins,
>> and blot out all my iniquities.

Three aspects of forgiveness are presented in these verses. First, the sinner needs to be purged and washed in order to be "whiter than snow." In Hebrew, images of sin were portrayed as red or scarlet because of the color of blood; for example, Isaiah prophesied, "Though your sins are like scarlet, / they shall be as white as snow; / though they are red like crimson, / they shall become like wool" (1:18). This conveyed the deadly aspect of sin. The point is that the sinner is changed by the act of forgiveness by a process of purification.

Second, the sinner feels the effects of this purification with "joy and gladness." Though the experience of guilt is compared to having one's bones crushed, the experience of forgiveness is a relief that brings deep joy. Usually this is a great surprise because the guilty person fears that God could not love a sinner. However, the admission of the truth of one's moral guilt brings a discovery that "God shows his love for us in that while we were yet sinners Christ died for us" (Romans 5:8). Therefore, "we also rejoice in God through our Lord Jesus Christ, through whom we have now received our reconciliation" (5:11). For a priest, the joy of hearing confessions is that so many people walk away from it with a sense of relief and deep joy.

Third, God "hides his face" from our sins and at the same time "blots" them out. The Father accepts the sacrifice for our sins that Jesus Christ effects on the cross, and he turns away from the reality of our sins so that he can see Christ reconciling us. At the same time, he is changing our sinful state in actuality by truly removing the sins. Verses 10-12 describe the state of spiritual restoration:

¹⁰Create in me a clean heart, O God,
and put a new and right spirit within me.

There is a double petition here, and each part helps us understand the other. First, the psalmist asks God to "create" a clean heart. Throughout the Bible, the only one who is the subject of the verb "create" is God: "God created the heavens and the earth" (Genesis 1:1), and "God created man in his own image" (1:27). The sinner's heart was darkened by sin, but God can create a new heart, as Ezekiel prophesied: "A new heart I will give you, and a new spirit I will put within you; and I will take out of your flesh the heart of stone and give you a heart of flesh. And I will put my spirit within you, and cause you to walk in my statutes and be careful to observe my ordinances" (36:26-27).

The idea of a new creation also appears in the New Testament: "Therefore, if any one is in Christ, he is a new creation; the old has passed away, behold, the new has come" (2 Corinthians 5:17). By attributing to Jesus Christ the power to create the believer anew, St. Paul is recognizing an important aspect of Christ's divinity. In Psalm 51, the prayers for forgiveness precede the prayer for a new heart. In the same way, the Christian's relationship with Christ begins with the faith that Jesus can bestow forgiveness of sins and reconciliation with God and then faith that Christ can make us new creations will take root and arise.

The next part of verse 10 asks God to "renew a steadfast spirit within me" (the literal translation of the Hebrew). This petition assumes that the psalmist had once been steadfast but, through his sin, had fallen away from that virtue. Here he asks God to "renew" that quality because he believes it is possible to be renewed. He does not despair of being virtuous again, although by expressing his hope in a prayer, he also recognizes that God will be the one who can make the change in the very depths of his spirit. He does not promise to accomplish this on his own because he depends on God's help and grace.

[11]Cast me not away from thy presence,
   and take not thy holy Spirit from me.

In the Second Book of Kings, when northern Israel is destroyed by the Assyrians, the Lord describes a long list of sins, especially sorcery, idolatry, and the sacrifice of children, as the reason he "cast them out of his sight" (17:20). God makes the same threat against Judah because of the idolatry, sins, and child sacrifice of King Manasseh (23:26-27). The petition here in Psalm 51 especially refers to being separated from worship in the Temple.

However, the second half of this petition prays that God not take his "holy Spirit from me," a reference to the intimate and personal relationship with God. The sinner desires and needs both the communal and liturgical worship of sacrifice and praise and the private and personal prayer that flows from a relationship with God's Holy Spirit. Consider this verse in light of St. Paul's teaching on slavery to sin and the necessity of the indwelling of the Holy Spirit (cf. Romans 7:14-25; 8:1-27).

[12]Restore to me the joy of thy salvation,
  and uphold me with a willing spirit.

The goal of the forgiveness of sins is not the mere absence of guilt but the transformation by which the reconciled person experiences the joy of the renewed relationship with God. He also asks God to "uphold" him, another way of expressing dependence on God. While he desires to have a "willing spirit" by which he freely gives of himself and chooses to do good, he also knows that willingness and freedom are God's gifts. A Christian can relate this verse to something St. Paul says in his Second Letter to the Corinthians: "Now the Lord is the Spirit, and where the Spirit of the Lord is, there is freedom" (3:17). Consider also Romans 8, where the Holy Spirit is also the one who frees people from slavery to sin (especially 8:15).

In the verses that follow, the psalmist promises to make reparation for his sins in a variety of ways. St. Paul writes, "For we are his workmanship, created in Christ Jesus for good works, which God prepared beforehand, that we should walk in them" (Ephesians 2:10). The good works result from God's new creation in Christ Jesus and are as much the fruit of God's grace as is the faith by which we believe and trust in him.

> [13]Then I will teach transgressors thy ways,
>   and sinners will return to thee.

The first step in the sinner's rehabilitation is a promise to teach other "transgressors" (rebels) and sinners so that they learn God's ways and return to him. Often, reformed sinners, including those recovering from addictions, are excellent at reaching out to people with the same weaknesses because they understand from the inside out the temptations and the logic of committing sin. A convicted Watergate conspirator, Charles Colson, experienced a conversion to a lived Christian faith and then did wonderful work in prison ministry until he died in 2012. The history of the Church is replete with penitents becoming great evangelists, such as St. Francis of Assisi or St. Ignatius of Loyola. As we pray this line, we can take extra time to ask our Lord what he might want to do with us to help other sinners, particularly with those to whom we can most easily relate our own experiences.

> [14]Deliver me from bloodguiltiness, O God,
>   thou God of my salvation,
>   and my tongue will sing aloud of thy deliverance.
> [15]O Lord, open thou my lips,
>   and my mouth shall show forth thy praise.

In these verses the psalmist promises to praise God as a result of deliverance from guilt. Of course, by his own nature, God does not need our praise. Instead, we can see this promise as an aspect of restoring the proper relationship of the creature to the Creator. Praise and adoration are the proper response to the realization that "he who is mighty has done great things for me" (Luke 1:49), just as awe and wonder are a proper response to seeing the Grand Canyon or the Canadian Rockies or other magnificent sites in nature. This response of praise expresses wonder at God's goodness and deeds, thereby improving us and our attitudes, just as appreciation of the works of Michelangelo, Beethoven, and other great artists increases our own sensitivity to beauty and goodness in creation.

> [16]For thou hast no delight in sacrifice;
>> were I to give a burnt offering, thou wouldst not be pleased.
> [17]The sacrifice acceptable to God is a broken spirit;
>> a broken and contrite heart, O God, thou wilt not despise.

The psalmist recognizes that the sacrifices offered at the Temple do not please God nearly as much as a "broken and contrite heart." This is a statement of profound faith, since many sinners fear that they can never please God again. However, it is precisely the contrite heart that admits sin and takes personal responsibility for it—as the psalmist has done throughout this psalm—that is the acceptable sacrifice to God. When we confess our sins in the Sacrament of Reconciliation or pray the penitential rite during Mass, we present not merely a psychological cleansing but a spiritual offering that is truly pleasing to God. Precisely at this point, many people experience great peace and joy in their relationship with God.

The psalm then concludes with petitions for the benefit of the community:

> [18]Do good to Zion in thy good pleasure;
>   rebuild the walls of Jerusalem,
> [19]then wilt thou delight in right sacrifices,
>   in burnt offerings and whole burnt offerings;
>   then bulls will be offered on thy altar.

The walls of Jerusalem were never destroyed in David's lifetime, as verse 18 says; they were destroyed about four hundred years later when the Babylonians destroyed the city in 587 B.C. For this reason, many scholars consider these verses an addition to the psalm after the exile as the nation repented of its communal sins and sought to rebuild the Temple and the whole city, beginning in 537 B.C.

Still, these verses bring out the communal perspective on repentance. Both the rebuilding of communal structures and the participation in communal worship are goods that can result from the repentance of the individual. The alcoholic or drug user who repents and changes his or her life can take a role in repairing the damage done to family relationships. Some recovering addicts do tremendous work in changing the larger society and fighting against the violence, theft, and murder that flow from drug use and destroy the rest of society. Each of us penitents can consider what we can do to repair the damage done to society by our sins and the sins of others and, in that way, live out this final prayer.

4. Psalm 130

Another lament of the individual contains a prayer for forgiveness, one which the Church prays on Wednesdays during Night Prayer in the Liturgy of the Hours. It is identified as a "Song of Ascents" because pilgrims to Jerusalem would sing it as they climbed the hills leading up to the sacred city.

> ¹Out of the depths I cry to thee, O LORD!
> ²Lord, hear my voice!
> Let thy ears be attentive
> to the voice of my supplications!

The psalm begins with a cry for help "out of the depths," without a description of the problem, as is true with the other laments. This vagueness allows anyone to pray it, whatever the reason for their experiencing the depths of pain, loneliness, confusion, or sin.

> ³If thou, O LORD, shouldst mark iniquities,
> Lord, who could stand?
> ⁴But there is forgiveness with thee,
> that thou mayest be feared.

These verses are an indirect petition for forgiveness that implies a confession of sin. The first motive for forgiveness is from the human perspective (verse 3): not one of us could stand if God marked out all our iniquities. Once again, we can see ourselves in the position of the unforgiving servant who was unable to pay the ten thousand talents his master had marked out for him (Matthew

18:24-27). The second motive is from God's perspective: he forgives us so that we may fear him (verse 4). Solomon's prayer at the dedication of the Temple includes a petition to "forgive, and act, and render to each whose heart thou knowest, according to all his ways . . . that they may fear thee all the days that they live in the land" (1 Kings 8:39-40). After the destruction of the city and the Temple in 587 B.C., the Lord promises through Jeremiah:

> [8]"I will cleanse them from all the guilt of their sin against me, and I will forgive all the guilt of their sin and rebellion against me. [9]And this city shall be to me a name of joy, a praise and a glory before all the nations of the earth who shall hear of all the good that I do for them; they shall fear and tremble because of all the good and all the prosperity I provide for it." (Jeremiah 33:8-9)

Jeremiah, too, sees the link between forgiveness of sin and the ability to fear. But note that the reason to "fear and tremble" is precisely "because of all the good and all the prosperity" the Lord will provide. Such fear is obviously a positive experience, so positive that fear is called "the beginning of wisdom" (Psalm 111:10; Proverbs 9:10; cf. Job 28:28; Proverbs 1:7) and "the whole duty of man" (Ecclesiastes 12:13). Many people confuse this positive sense of "fear" (*yirah*) of the Lord with different Hebrew words meaning "dread" (*pahad*) or "terror" (*'emah, magor,* or *behalah*), which God's enemies experience because they oppose him (cf. Exodus 15:16; 23:27; Deuteronomy 11:25; Psalm 31:13; 53:5; 78:33; Isaiah 2:19, 21; and various other texts). These latter words are almost always negative experiences, but "fear of

the Lord" has many positive contexts in which it is both a virtue among humans and a gift of the Holy Spirit (cf. Isaiah 11:2).

The rest of Psalm 130 expresses confidence that God's word
of forgiveness will come as certainly as the dawn:

> [5]I wait for the LORD, my soul waits,
>   and in his word I hope;
> [6]my soul waits for the LORD
>   more than watchmen for the morning,
>   more than watchmen for the morning.
> [7]O Israel, hope in the LORD!
>   For with the Lord there is steadfast love,
>   and with him is plenteous redemption.
> [8]And he will redeem Israel
>   from all his iniquities.

Ultimately, this confidence lies in Israel's understanding of the
nature of the Lord, namely, that he is full of covenant love and
redemption (verse 7). Redemption is not offered stingily but plen-
teously, because the Lord has an abundance of mercy with which
to redeem Israel from iniquities. The verb "redeem" (*padah*) is
usually associated with family obligations to avenge the murder
of a family member, retrieve a family member who was enslaved,
or buy back property that had been sold to someone outside the
family. Its use in the Bible indicates that the Lord is willing to
take on family responsibilities for his people by redeeming them
from the iniquities they commit. The word "iniquities" (`*avon*
in Hebrew) comes from a root meaning "bent." These iniquities
bend, distort, and misshape Israel, while the Lord's redemption

and forgiveness restore the repentant to his proper image and likeness of God.

No matter how deeply a person has fallen into sin and iniquity, this psalm offers hope that the Lord can reach into those depths and draw the sinner out so as to bring redemption. God's concern lies more with his desire to save sinners than with counting the sins they have committed.

5. Psalm 32

In Psalm 51:14-15, the penitent promises to praise the Lord for the forgiveness of sins. Two psalms, Psalm 32 and Psalm 103, were written to express thanksgiving and praise after the forgiveness has been received. These would have been prayed after a sin offering or guilt offering was accepted in the Temple. The modern penitent can pray these psalms after receiving the Sacrament of Reconciliation, especially if it has been a long time since the preceding Confession and if this experience of reconciliation opens the way to reception of the other sacraments again.

Psalm 32 is a "Maskil," a noun derived from a verb meaning to be "prudent" and perhaps meaning "a contemplative poem" or a melody that is skillfully played.

¹Blessed is he whose transgression is forgiven,
    whose sin is covered.
²Blessed is the man to whom the LORD imputes no
    iniquity,
    and in whose spirit there is no deceit.

The psalm begins by declaring a double beatitude for the sinner whose transgression (rebellion) and sin are forgiven. Verse 2 intensifies the beatitude by describing the repentant sinner as someone in whom there is no deceit. This implies that he has not hidden any sins during his confession to God but has been forthright about his guilt and iniquity. The term "covered" (*kisseh*) means "forgiven." Its use is derived from the idea that the blood of the animal sacrifice in a guilt or sin offering "covers" the sin, and it is forgiven. A similar idea appears in the New Testament in passages that describe Christians having their sins forgiven by the blood of Jesus (cf. Hebrews 12:24; 1 Peter 1:2, 19; Revelation 1:5; 5:9; 7:14), a doctrine rooted in Jesus' own words at the Last Supper: "Drink of it, all of you; for this is my blood of the covenant, which is poured out for many for the forgiveness of sins" (Matthew 26:27-28). The Christian can connect the psalm's beatitude of having sins covered for forgiveness to the saving death of Jesus Christ on the cross.

> ³When I declared not my sin, my body wasted away
> through my groaning all day long.
> ⁴For day and night thy hand was heavy upon me;
> my strength was dried up as by the heat
> of summer. [*Selah*]
> ⁵I acknowledged my sin to thee,
> and I did not hide my iniquity;
> I said, "I will confess my transgressions to the LORD";
> then thou didst forgive the guilt of my sin. [*Selah*]

These verses describe the experience of many people who try to keep the fact of their sinful behavior to themselves. While this translation says, "My body wasted away," a more literal translation of the Hebrew is "My bones grew old / wasted away." The bones are the most enduring physical part of the body, lasting centuries after the flesh is gone. If they are aging or wasting away, the root problem must be very serious. Some diseases certainly affect the bones, but the psalmist identifies his problem as moral.

The psalmist not only feels the effects of his interior turmoil due to sin, but God's "hand was heavy upon me," sapping him of strength. Some people, especially those who once had a good relationship with God, often feel the absence of God as a very heavy burden. They may try to hide the absence from themselves, but the hollowness causes spiritual desolation. Only when he "acknowledged" his sin and iniquity by confessing his transgressions to the Lord did he find forgiveness of his guilt. As is the point of Psalm 51, honest confession and admission of guilt bring a penitent true peace.

> ⁶Therefore let every one who is godly
>   offer prayer to thee;
> at a time of distress, in the rush of great waters,
>   they shall not reach him.
> ⁷Thou art a hiding place for me,
>   thou preservest me from trouble;
>   thou dost encompass me with deliverance. [*Selah*]

The confession of sin leads to faith that God will save from danger those who pray to him. In verse 7, the psalmist offers the more personal witness that God is a "hiding place" for him and that he preserves and delivers him.

The next verses are a prophetic statement in which the Lord answers the psalmist in words spoken through the priest or a Temple prophet:

> ⁸I will instruct you and teach you
>   the way you should go;
>   I will counsel you with my eye upon you.
> ⁹Be not like a horse or a mule, without understanding,

which must be curbed with bit and bridle,
  else it will not keep with you.

The Lord promises to "instruct," "teach," and "counsel" the psalmist on the path he should take as he leaves his sinful ways. The first step of repentance is the realization that you are on the wrong path, a path that leads to death. In the second step, you retrace your steps and move away from that path. Finally, you follow the good and true path of God. The Lord promises that he will not only offer the guidance along this path of holiness, but that his eye will be "upon you," a way to indicate the Lord's personal presence in the life of the sinner. Psalm 51:10-12 understood this presence in terms of the Lord's own Spirit upholding the penitent. In both cases, the presence of the Lord is necessary to sustain the new way of life.

The negative admonition warns against being "like a horse" or mule that is led by "bit and bridle." Such animals have no understanding; they follow their instincts. Humans can understand that the Lord's way is good and right, so they can use their free will to choose correctly and, as Psalm 51:12 says, with a "willing spirit."

Then the psalmist responds to the prophetic words with a wisdom reflection of his own:

[10]Many are the pangs of the wicked;
  but steadfast love surrounds him who trusts in
    the LORD.

This is a reflection on the psalmist's own experience and of others' experiences of the way life is. Therefore, the hearer is to conclude that he should turn from sin and trust in the Lord. Steadfast "covenant love" will surround the virtuous person who trusts God.

The psalmist concludes with a summons for the community to rejoice with him in his forgiven state, similar to the ending of Psalm 51:

> [11]Be glad in the LORD, and rejoice, O righteous,
>   and shout for joy, all you upright in heart!

All three verbs—"be glad," "rejoice," and "shout for joy"—and the nouns "righteous" and "upright" are in the plural form in Hebrew, indicating the communal nature of the celebration. This psalm would have been sung and prayed in the Temple, probably at a sacrificial offering. There is a communal aspect of reconciliation with God, even when an individual sinner is reconciled. The Church continues to celebrate reconciliation, both in the Sacrament of Reconciliation and in the Eucharist. And just as the psalmist rejoices in God's mercy, so should we.

6. Psalm 103

This psalm is a hymn in which the psalmist is addressing himself in a personal prayer that draws on God's faithfulness to his people throughout the history of Israel. It is attributed to David.

> [1]Bless the LORD, O my soul;
> and all that is within me, bless his holy name!
> [2]Bless the LORD, O my soul,
> and forget not all his benefits,

Usually hymns summon the whole community to worship, but in this hymn, the psalmist addresses his own soul, commanding it to "bless the Lord." This command is repeated in verse 2 and again at the conclusion in verses 20-22 to highlight the solemnity of the command. The command to "forget not all [the Lord's] benefits" opens the introduction to the next verses, in which many of the Lord's benefits are recounted.

> [3]who forgives all your iniquity,
> who heals all your diseases,

The first benefit is the forgiveness of iniquity (the term derived from being "bent"), and immediately following is the healing of disease. This is not unlike Psalm 32:3-5, where the confession of sin is closely connected with the healing of the bodily disorders that resulted from sin.

⁴who redeems your life from the Pit,
    who crowns you with steadfast love and mercy,

The "Pit" refers to the place of the dead. One method of burial among the ancients was to place a body in a cave for a year and then gather the bones and throw them into a pit. Not only does the Lord save the man from death, but he "crowns" him with "steadfast love and mercy."

⁵who satisfies you with good as long as you live
    so that your youth is renewed like the eagle's.

The satisfaction with "good" throughout life works as a renewal of youth. Some people who find satisfaction at each stage of life are able to maintain a youthful quality. People who constantly long for what they do not yet have or no longer possess tend to age more rapidly because their discontent makes them constantly upset and worried.

⁶The Lord works vindication
    and justice for all who are oppressed.

The "vindication" that the Lord works is a translation of the word usually meaning "righteousness" (*tzedaqah*), while "justice" is derived from the word meaning "judgment." These terms were commonly used in the courts of law to indicate the verdict of the person who was in the legal right and to define the just impartiality of the proceedings. Even when human courts and judges are unrighteous, the Lord will protect the innocent.

A Christian might take some cues from the New Testament to consider this verse in terms of the final judgment of the soul. Jesus (1 John 2:1) and the Holy Spirit (John 14:16, 26; 15:26; 16:7) are both called "Paraclete," a term that means "counselor" or "advocate" in the way that people use these terms for defense lawyers. When we are united to Jesus and the Holy Spirit of truth dwells in us, they act as our defense lawyers. The Greek word *diabolos*, from which comes the English word "devil," means a prosecuting attorney, and the Hebrew "Satan" means "accuser." We can understand the judgment of the soul as a courtroom in which the devil accuses us of our sins while Jesus and the Holy Spirit plead our case and the Father is the Judge. How great it is to have the Judge's Son as our defense attorney!

The next verses relate to the history of salvation:

⁷He made known his ways to Moses,
       his acts to the people of Israel.
⁸The LORD is merciful and gracious,
       slow to anger and abounding in steadfast love.
⁹He will not always chide,
       nor will he keep his anger for ever.

God "made known his ways" to Moses and Israel, and these truths remain the deposit of revelation for the psalmist as well. Verse 8 recalls the great confession of faith when the Lord revealed himself to Moses on Mount Sinai and proclaimed his core personal qualities, including his willingness to let go of his justified anger and forgive Israel (Exodus 34:6-7). Remember that this revelation to Moses took place immediately after the nation had made and worshiped the golden calf, thereby breaking the first commandment. The episode of the golden calf and the other sins of the nation of Israel are close to the psalmist's mind, but so is the Lord's constant mercy:

> [10]He does not deal with us according to our sins,
>> nor requite us according to our iniquities.
> [11]For as the heavens are high above the earth,
>> so great is his steadfast love toward those who fear him;
> [12]as far as the east is from the west,
>> so far does he remove our transgressions from us.

The psalmist begins these verses with a statement of principle: if God dealt with us according to our sins and iniquities, we would suffer the fate of the people at the time of the flood. Rather, his steadfast covenant love (*hesed*) is as high as the heavens, and he removes our sins from us "as far as the east is from the west." Neither his covenant love nor his merciful forgiveness is deserved, but the Lord bestows them anyway.

> [13]As a father pities his children,
>> so the LORD pities those who fear him.
> [14]For he knows our frame;
>> he remembers that we are dust.

The psalmist turns from the grand images of extraordinary height and breadth to the tender image of God as a Father who pities his children, whose frailty he knows well. After the cosmic images of mercy and forgiveness, the psalmist takes comfort in the gentle and tender image of fatherly love as the basis for forgiveness of sin. Of course, Jesus brings us to the same understanding in the Our Father.

Next, the psalmist offers his own reflections on human frailty in contrast to God's greatness:

> [15]As for man, his days are like grass;
>   he flourishes like a flower of the field;
> [16]for the wind passes over it, and it is gone,
>   and its place knows it no more.

In Israel the rains come only between November and March. During the dry season between April and November, the grasses and flowers of the field dry up completely and die. Reflecting on this fact of life in Israel, the psalmist considers that all humanity dies. With very few exceptions, individuals are no longer remembered by history and pass from our memories.

> [17]But the steadfast love of the LORD is from everlasting
>   to everlasting
>   upon those who fear him,
>   and his righteousness to children's children,
> [18]to those who keep his covenant
>   and remember to do his commandments.
> [19]The LORD has established his throne in the heavens,
>   and his kingdom rules over all.

In contrast to history, the Lord's steadfast covenant love and righteousness are eternal for those who fear him and keep his covenant by doing his commandments. These verses contain one of the few hints of eternal life in the Old Testament. This hint is not developed but lingers as a mystery. The statement of faith that the Lord's throne is in heaven and that "his kingdom rules over all" is a way to form a basis and support for the hope of everlasting love and righteousness. The unraveling of this mystery into an understanding of the kingdom of God as a promise of eternal life with the Father in heaven will be presented by Jesus Christ in the Gospels. This psalm is a good way to prayerfully consider how much further Jesus' promises take us.

The conclusion of Psalm 103 connects the individual with the heavenly host:

> [20]Bless the LORD, O you his angels,
>> you mighty ones who do his word,
>> hearkening to the voice of his word!
> [21]Bless the LORD, all his hosts,
>> his ministers that do his will!
> [22]Bless the LORD, all his works,
>> in all places of his dominion.
> Bless the LORD, O my soul!

The psalmist senses that his worship is united with all of heaven and earth. He summons the angels, who are always obedient to God's command and word, to bless the Lord. The "hosts" and "ministers" are the stars, sun, and moon, and the forces of nature that also obey the Lord. The rest of the works of the Lord are all other things in creation, and the psalmist summons them to praise the Lord. Psalm 148 and Daniel 3:29-68 are examples of hymns in which all creatures—angels, heavenly bodies, natural forces, earth, animals, and people—are summoned to "bless the Lord." Verse 22 concludes this hymn with the same summons to the individual's soul to bless the Lord with which the psalm began. Having reflected on all that God has done to forgive, heal, and redeem each person, this personal act of praise is the appropriate response.

Also by Fr. Mitch Pacwa, SJ

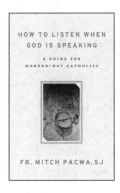

How to Listen When God Is Speaking
A Guide for Modern-Day Catholics

"In *How to Listen When God Is Speaking*, Fr. Mitch Pacwa challenges Catholics to embrace their fundamental vocation: to be a listener. In the best of the Ignatian tradition, he teaches us to hear God's voice—above the noise we encounter each day—and take it to heart. This book is a real gift for our spiritual lives. I recommend it for all readers."
—Cardinal Timothy M. Dolan,
Archbishop of New York

"Pope Benedict XVI liked to remind us that a priest is a man of God. In Fr. Pacwa's book, a man of God introduces us to God so that we can listen to him well. This is a book helpful to both the friends of God and those still distant from him."
—Cardinal Francis George,
Archbishop of Chicago
176 pages, 5¼ x 8, softcover, Item# BLTGE0

Fr. Mitch's website can be found at www.fathermitchpacwa.org.

the WORD
among us®
The *Spirit* of Catholic Living

T his book was published by The Word Among Us. Since 1981, The Word Among Us has been answering the call of the Second Vatican Council to help Catholic laypeople encounter Christ in the Scriptures.

The name of our company comes from the prologue to the Gospel of John and reflects the vision and purpose of all of our publications: to be an instrument of the Spirit, whose desire is to manifest Jesus' presence in and to the children of God. In this way, we hope to contribute to the Church's ongoing mission of proclaiming the gospel to the world so that all people would know the love and mercy of our Lord and grow ever more deeply in love with him.

Our monthly devotional magazine, *The Word Among Us*, features meditations on the daily and Sunday Mass readings, and currently reaches more than one million Catholics in North America and another half million Catholics in one hundred countries around the world. Our book division, The Word Among Us Press, publishes numerous books, Bible studies, and pamphlets that help Catholics grow in their faith.

To learn more about who we are and what we publish, log on to our website at www.wau.org. There you will find a variety of Catholic resources that will help you grow in your faith.

Embrace His Word, Listen to God . . .

www.wau.org